Martha Keldgord's Journal

1911 – 1930

Family, Friends, Church and
Farm in Rural Harlan, Iowa

Martha Keldgord's Journal

1911 – 1930

Family, Friends, Church and Farm in Rural Harlan, Iowa

Compiled and Published by Bob Mesenbrink

2014

ISBN 978-0-9916181-0-1

Published by Bob Mesenbrink, 2014; Arvada, Colorado, USA.
http://www.mesenbrinks.com

Cover Photo: The photo on the cover is a portrait of Martha Keldgord taken around 1914 or 1915. The photographer has not been identified.

Contents

Martha Keldgord's Journal 1911 - 1930

Preface

When I first glanced at this journal, I knew it was precious. This journal is from the early 1900s, a period my own parents were born into, a period that I studied in school as "modern" history. So it's not that it's particularly old. And its writer, Martha Keldgord, is somebody that I remember. My wife knew her as "Grandma Larsen". It's not as if it was written by a historical figure. This journal is precious because it's about family, friends and neighbors, and the otherwise forgotten details of their lives.

At its bare bones, genealogy is a collection of names, dates, places and relationships. But really, genealogy is about knowing one's ancestors. That is not an easy task after those ancestors are gone. To know ones ancestors, or anybody for that matter, requires more than dates and places. It requires an understanding of how they lived, who they associated with, why they lived where they did, why they moved (or stayed), and what they struggled with. That's what puts the "meat on the bones" of genealogy. But that information is very hard to come by. We know our parents and grandparents as little more than just that - our parents and grandparents. We know less about their lives before we came into the picture. Once they are gone from us, we can't ask them. A journal such as this one helps answer questions that we should have asked years ago.

Martha's journal provides a bit of that information, not just for her family, but for her church, neighbors, and community. She doesn't provide opinions or feelings about what happens - just facts. So her journal doesn't directly answer the "why" questions. But those facts include the events that affected regular people around her and give us a glimpse into what life was like for her and those around her.

I am very grateful to Martha for taking the time to write down her daily activities and I hope readers will benefit from her journal. In addition, I would like to thank Elliott and Norma Larsen for preserving this journal over the years, my wife, Irene, for her support and editing help, and Elliott, Carolyn, Joyce, Joan, and Terry for their permission to publish the journal and family photos.

Introduction

Martha Keldgord was born April 4, 1895 in Shelby County, Iowa. Her parents were Jacob Keldgord (originally Kjeldgaard) and Martine Nelson (originally Nielsen), both Danish immigrants.

Jacob had come over in 1875 with his parents, Peder Christensen Keldgord and Marianne (Jacobsdatter/Jacobsen) Keldgord, and his siblings, settling in Shelby County, Iowa.

Martine came over much later than Jacob, in 1891. She had at least three siblings that immigrated, but at different times. Martine married Jacob soon after her arrival. The Kjeldgaards and Nielsens were both from near Løgstør, Denmark and likely knew each other quite well, although Jacob was thirteen years older than Martine.

Martha had a sister, Mabel, who was just a year older, and a brother Oscar, who was six years younger. Another sister, Olga, had died in 1904. Martha's father died in 1912, and sister Mabel married in 1914 moving away in 1920. So much of this journal is about Martha, Oscar, and their mother, and their life on the farm in Center Township of Shelby County, Iowa.

Martha mentioned other relatives. Jacob's brother, Chris Keldgord, lived in an adjacent farm. He had died before this journal was begun, but his children, cousins of Martha, were still around. Also, Martha had second cousins on the Keldgord side who visited each other.

Other relatives are mentioned on the Nelson side. Most notably was Martha's uncle, Reverend Nels Nelson, who held offices in the Danish Baptist Conference of America and served various Danish Baptist congregations.

This journal was started in 1912, although it records a few events from 1911. It goes through 1923, with single entries for 1926, 1927 and 1930. Dates are almost always recorded with each entry. But the entries are not always recorded in chronological order, so some events are recorded after-the-fact. The 1911 entries are probably copied from an earlier journal.

Jacob and Martine were both Danish immigrants and Baptists. The Baptist movement in Denmark started and grew during the 1800s. The Keldgords were members of Altamont Baptist Church (Cuppy's Grove), one of the first Danish Baptist churches in the country, but frequented the Danish Baptist church in Harlan as well. Numerous church events, in various area churches, and various pastors, were mentioned throughout the journal. Many of their friends were also members of the Altamont Baptist Church.

Harlan was the main town for them, although they made trips to Walnut to see friends and family. Their farm was located in Section 27 in southern Center Township. From their farm, Harlan was about two miles north and three miles west. Altamont Baptist Church was about four miles south, in Monroe Township. Walnut was about eight miles south and one mile east, on the northern edge of Pottawattamie County. Martha frequently mentioned going "up" to Harlan or "down" to Cuppy's Grove or Walnut.

Most of Martha's journal discussed fairly routine, daily events. Weather was mentioned nearly every entry. The repeating annual cycle of farm life is very apparent with thawing snow, muddy roads and spring rains, field work, planting the garden and crops, raising baby pigs and chickens, gathering eggs, picking and canning fruit and berries, making hay, canning vegetables, picking corn, and then frost, snow and blizzards. But scattered throughout are the names and events of friends and family in her life.

She often mentioned prices, in the purchase of household and farm goods, and in the sale of canned goods, eggs, grain, and farm animals. And major events such as World War I, the 1918 Influenza epidemic, automobiles, radio, airplanes and hot air balloons are all mentioned to varying degrees.

Martha is not the only writer in the journal. Since she is mentioned by name in a few spots and the handwriting varies, it is clear that Mabel, Oscar, and Martine added an occasional entry.

Although the journal is in good condition, some of the writing is faint, due to age and frequent use of pencil. In addition, Martha didn't use the best grammar or punctuation. Her spelling, especially of names, varied quite a bit, making transcription difficult. None of the original spelling or grammatical errors are marked. It is possible that the editor's own errors have crept in, but hopefully nothing that takes away from the original intent. Additions by the editor are indicated in square brackets. Footnotes are used to explain and add details. Martha's entries about deaths are supported with references to the gravestone records found at www.findagrave.com.

There are two indices. One is an index to places and the other is an index to people. Because there is such variability in name spelling, some common name spellings have been combined. For example, both Petersons and Petersens are listed under Peterson/en in the index. Lesser used names with multiple spellings are listed in the index under a single, corrected, spelling. Since Martha, Mabel, Oscar and their mother, Martine, are frequently mentioned, they are not listed in the index.

The bold page number headings in the journal indicate the page number of the original journal. Often, the original journal included "Memorial" or the year or similar headings. Several pages of recipes and poems are omitted from the journal as noted.

The Cover and First Page

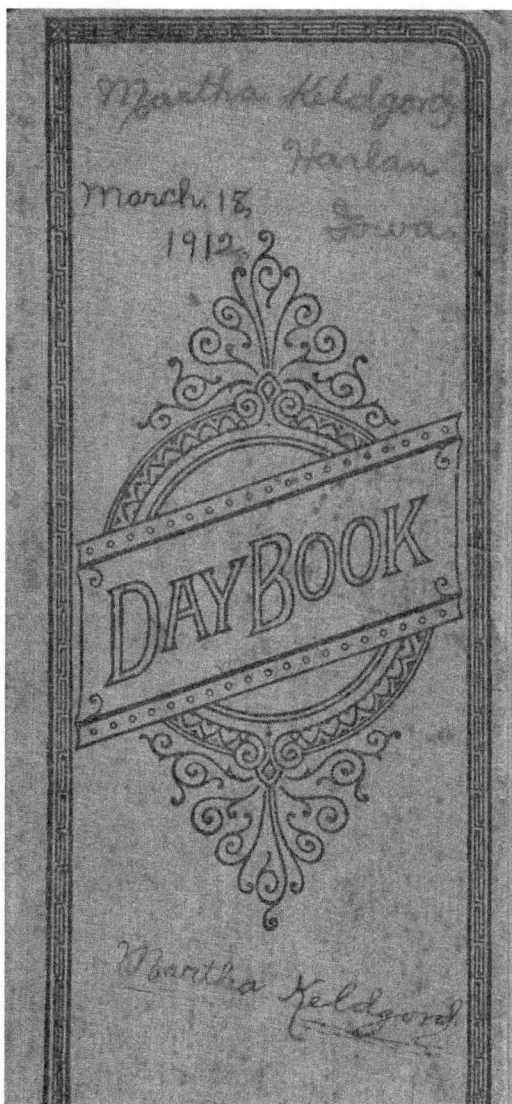

1912/1911

Page 1

March 18th 1912 – Mamma and Papa were to town to day with Andrews. I got my new blue skirt.

March 18, 1912 – We bought 6 sacks of white flour of Poole.

March 19, 1912 – The creek [1] down here is overflowing. It is clear up to the bridge.

March 19, 1912 – Esther [2] [Kemp] and I took the examination from common school, Feb. 20, 21, 1912.

**Jacob Keldgord and Martine Nelsen – 1891
(Photo by Dammand.)**

March 20, 1912 – To-day is the 20th day of March, 1912. There isn't any school to-day because it is snowing and drifting.

---

[1] The creek ran from north to south through the west side of the length of Keldgord's 80 acres.
[2] There was an Esther Kemp who was nearly the same age and a neighbor to the east. A poem in the back of the journal was signed "Esther Kemp".

March 21, 1912 – Bergs [3] were at our place March 21, 1912. They brought our bobsled.

March 23, 1912 – We were all to town to but Ma. We stopped in to Baak's.[4] It was Mary's birthday. 15 years. We went the first time in [Berg's sled?].

June – The strawberries are ripe June 3 to 13th, 1911.

The wild gooseberries are big enough to pick, June 14, 1911.

Our white roses are in bloom, June 14, 1911.

Our red astricons[?] and yellow crabs are ripe and black berries, July 28, 1911.

Hans Benson's and Pete Petersen were at our place to-day and so was Clarence, Sept 14, 1911.

Page 2

Jan. 26, 1911 – Mrs. Soren Miller died to-day in Harlan, age 73 years.

Anna Keldgord [5] and Claude Marvin were married Sept. 14, 1911 in Alma.

We got our corn picked Nov. 3, 1911.

We were out to Bergs on Chris Nelson's [6] place Nov. 10, 1911.

It is very cold to-day Nov. 12, 1911, 5 of our hens froze to death.

---

[3] The 1910 Federal Census shows N. A. Berg and wife, Anna, of Fairview twp. to have children: Grace, Mabel, Howard, Gordon, Henry, and Earl.
[4] The Baaks have not been identified.
[5] Anna Keldgord was a cousin, daughter of Martha's uncle Chris Keldgord.
[6] There was a Chris Nelson farm south of Keldgord's in Monroe Twp.

Knud Hansen died 28th Nov 1911.

To-day is a snow storm, the 2nd of March 1912.

Mabel and Martha Keldgord
(No photographer identified.)

To-day is the last day of March, the 31st, 1912. It thundered and lightening last night. It was the first spring rain. It is Sunday. We are going to stay home to-day. I am reading Elsie's Motherhood. Mabel is reading Donald and Dorthy. It is kind of cold to-day. We went over to Andrew's to-day.

To-day was my birthday, April 4, 1912. 17 yrs old. It has been very windy. I got 4 postals.

To-day is April 6, 1912. It is chilly and the wind is in the northwest. It is raining very hard.

Yesterday we got 55 eggs in, April 9, 1912.

We are at home to-day. It is very windy and cloudy. Martha is sick and so is Mabel. It is the 14th of April 1912. [Since both Martha and Mabel are mentioned by name, this was probably written by their mother, Martine Nelson Keldgord.]

Anna Knudsen & James Andersen were married April 10, 1912.

Page 3 Memorial

We were out to Berg's [7] 1st time yesterday April 27, 1912. We saw four trains go by their place. I got my birthday present the same day.

To-day Sunday May 5, 1912. It is very nice weather. I am all alone home, the rest are in church. The plum and cherry trees are covered with blossoms. We have a few apples left.

To-day is Saturday May 11, 1912. Our lilacs are in bloom and it is misting. It rained last night. Findlays planted corn yesterday.

We sold 2 pigs the 18th of May 1912. 7.15 a cwt.

We washed the first time in our new washing machine 18th May 1912.

Sena is making Mabel's new lawn dress to-day. Aug. 28, 1912.

To-day is nice weather. Our plums are laying thick on the ground. And the cucumbers are getting yellow. I have made plum jelly to-day and it is getting stiff already. I have also churned by myself and got about 8 lbs of butter. Monday, Sept. 2, 1912.

Page 4 Memorial

Sept. 7, 1912 – Mamma and Mabel come home from Chicago yesterday Sept 7, 1912. [8] We visited at M. Christensen's. I got my locket and chain, and my pin and back comb, pillow slips. [Mabel's handwriting].

---

[7] Railroads ran north and south through Harlan along the western edge of Center Township, giving a clue as to where the Bergs went.
[8] They were possibly visiting Martine's brother, Rev. Nels Nelson who was serving at First Danish Baptist Church in Chicago.

Oct. 23, 1912 – Oct. 23. Papa and Mabel went to town with 24 spring roosters and one hen. They weighed 105 lbs. & 9 ½ ₵ a lbs. $10.50 for them.

In Sept we sold 20 spring roosters and 4 old hens. We got $11.15 for them. It was 12 ½ ₵.

Oct. 23, 1912 – I bought my pillow slips & my big doily & handkerchief cloth & my new shoes.

Oct. 18, 1912 – We got our new broom Oct. 18, 1912.

Nov. 28, 1912 – Bergs were out to our place for Thanksgiving dinner. The weather was a little cool.

Nov. 29, 1912 – Friday. We are all home and the weather is just beautiful to-day, the wind is in the west. We are going to town tomorrow if it is nice.

Nov. 28, 1912 – Papa sold Mamma's cow to C Stofferson to-day for $36.00.

Page 5 Memorial

Dec 1912 – We were out to Berg's Dec. 25, 1912. The boys went skating.

Martha Keldgord's Journal 1911 - 1930

1913

Jan 18, 1913 – P. Paulsons & Mrs. Krogh and Back's were up to our place. It was nice weather.

Jan. 12, 1913 – Our new church was dedicated the 12th of Jan 1913. There were about 450 people there.

Jan. 10, 1913 – Old Kate was shot the 10th of Jan. 1913.

**Jacob Keldgord 1848 – 1913
(Photo by Dammand)**

Jan. 23, 1913 – To-day is my birthday. It is very nice weather, but very muddy. I rec'd 7 postals. [This would be Mabel's entry as she was born 23 January 1893.]

Jan. 31, 1913 – It is very cold & frosty to-day. The wind is in the northwest. We are not going after Martha to-day.

Jan. 26, 1913 – Last Sunday we had visitors. W. Bisgaard's [9] came up to see us.

Feb. 21, 1913 – Papa [10] died Feb 21, 1913 and was buried the 25 of Feb. 1913. Uncle Nels [11] and Mrs. C.E. Marvin were present at the funeral.

---

[9] Willads Bisgaard lived in Walnut. His wife was sister to Mabel's (and Martha's) future husband, Walter Larsen.
[10] Jacob Pedersen Keldgord (Kjeldgaard), b. 4 June 1848, Skræm, Øster Han, Hjørring, Denmark.
[11] Nels Nelson was Martine's brother. He was a Baptist preacher.

Page 6

Mar. 2, 1913 – To-day is very cold & frosty. But wind is in the south.

March 13, 1913 – We butchered last Tuesday and is putting the meat away to-day. It rained and thundered and lighting last night for the first time this spring.

March 15, 1913 – To-day it is snow all over the ground, and the trees are covered. It was nearly a blizzard last night.

Mar. 22, 1913 – To-day it is a little cold but the wind is in the southeast. We got 50 eggs in to-day

Reverend Nels Nelsen
(Photo by A. Holm)

and we have set a hen. She will hatch out the 8th of April.

Mar. 23, 1913 – Yesterday was Easter Sunday. We were down to Bisgaard's for dinner. In the evening there came up a wind storm, and thundered and lightning and poured down rain. Over west it tore the roofs off of houses & barns and moved small buildings.

Page 7

Mar. 25, 1913 – To-day it is snowing a little. We have already 8 or 10 little pigs.

April 1, 1913 – To-day is very nice weather, we ironed to-day and we are going to sew a little too. We have 16 little pigs some of then a week old to-day.

April 4, 1913 18 yrs old – It was very nice weather but a little muddy. Bergs & Mabel C[hristensen], and Bertha, Dena & Charlie were over here. I got about a dozen postals. A pin from Mamma. A perfume bottle from Bergs. A cup & saucer from M.C.

April 6, 1913 – We were to church Sunday, and down to Arentsen's after. Mabel, Walter [12], and I were to church at night. We got in 74 eggs that night.

Mar. 30, 1913 – Harry Sahl [13] got hurt the 30th of March. He has now been sick a week 6 of April.

Page 8

April 10, 1913 – To-day is very dark weather, and has been for four days and to-day it is snowing. We have already 5 or 6 little chickens.

April 13, 1913 Sun. – To-day it is very warm and we were all to church to-day. We wore our spring coats and summer hats the first time this year.

April 14 Mon. – To-day we ironed and baked white bread and Mamma and Oscar went to town in the lumber wagon. We ironed on our oil stove the first time this year. We are going to clean house this week.

April 12 – Oscar got his new hat the 12th of April. We also got our hats, mine trimmed.

F.F. [Forest Findlay] is seeding to-day. W.F.[Walter Findlay] [14] finished planting our corn to-day, May 12, 1913.

---

[12] Walter is Walter Larsen of Walnut. He married Mabel and later would marry Martha.
[13] Sahls were neighbors to the west.

Oscar Keldgord (1945)
(family photo)

Page 9

April 23, 1913 – It is blowing very hard to-day and has been since the 20th. We are sewing our gray aprons to-day. Yesterday we sewed my blue apron and our new corset covers.

April 30, 1913 – We are all going out to R. J. Rasmussen's[15] to-day. And maybe Martha is going to stay out there a while. It is blowing a little to-day. [This and the next entry appear to be written by Martine.]

April 28, 1913 – Monday was Arbor day. We planted 10 trees, and our potatoes too. Our radishes are up and lettuce too.

May 4, 1913 – We are alone home to-day. Oscar, and I, and Mamma. It is very muddy, it rained yesterday. [Rev. Peter] C. Larsen will preach his farewell sermon to-day. Martha is out by R. J. Rasmussens now. [This and the next entry appear to be written by Mabel.]

May 4 – We have got 16 little chickens and 14 hens setting.

May 4, 1913 – The apple and plum trees are full of blossoms. [The next entry, perhaps two lines of the page are torn off.]

Page 10

[Entry at top of page has been erased.]

---

[14] Findlays were neighbors and rented the Keldgord land for a time.
[15] R. J. Rasmussens lived near Jacksonville, about eight miles to the northeast.

May 5, 1913 – Mabel got her new shoes for summer yesterday. And Oscar his new summer cap too.

May 12, 1913 – To-day we washed. It is awful warm, we have got almost 40 little chickens.

May 12, 1913 – Our lilics are in bloom now. We have used quite a lot of our pie plants.

May 14, 1913 – Last Thursday morning the river down here was over its banks almost up to Chris Hansen's and up to Mike's farm[16].

May 18, 1913 – Yesterday was Sunday. We were to church in the morning and over to Andrew's for dinner. [Rev.] Jacob [Olsen] from South Dakota preached. [This and the next entry appear to be written by Mabel.]

May 19, 1913 – Martha and I had a letter from Amy Taylor [17] last Saturday

May 20, 1913 – To-day is Tuesday. It has rained all day till now and it is now almost noon.

Page 11

April 22, 1913 – Alma Taylor was married the 22nd of April to Mr. Will Stall.

May 21, 1913 – To-day is Wednesday. It is dark and cloudy. We have got 50 little chickens and 9 hens setting.

---

[16] The 1911 Atlas of Shelby County Iowa shows a C. Hansen and Michael Christiansen with land along the Nishnabotna River, just a mile east of Keldgords.

[17] Albert and Alice Taylor were just two houses away on the 1900 census and had daughters Amy and Alma. They had moved to Minnesota by 1910.

May 24, 1913 – It is Saturday to-day. And is very nice weather. We have got 81 little chickens and some hatching to-day.

July 14, 1913 – Ras bought Nels Erickson [18] farm to-day. I got my new white dress washed the first time.

Aug. 5, 1913 – To-day is a little cloudy and hope it will rain, as we have not had any rain for quite a while.

Aug. 16, 1913 – Mabel finished embroidering Mamma's pillow slips to-day. We are starting our bureau scarfs to-day.

Sept. 1, 1913 – To-day is very nice weather. We are going to wash and the school starts to-day too. I am going out to work at Bisgaards to-day.

Page 12

Sept. 28, 1913 – Yesterday was Sunday but it was very rainy and muddy. We stayed all alone home all day.

Willads Bisgaard Family – 1911 - Clockwise from left: Sophie Larsen Bisgaard, Willads Bisgaard, Einer, Pete (in center), Arnold, Edna (baby). (No photographer identified.)

Oct. 29, 1913 – We had the cows in the barn last night the first time this fall. We are washing to-day. It is very cold and cloudy. [Probably Martine's entry.]

---

[18] According to the 1911 Atlas of Shelby County Iowa, there was a Nels Erickson farm one mile west of Jacksonville.

Oct. 28, 1913 - It snowed yesterday. We got the cows in the first piece of stalks yesterday. [Probably Martine's entry.]

Nov. 4, 1913 – I came home from Frank Hansen's Tuesday after staying their 4 wks.

Nov. 6, 1913 – We took the plasterers in to-night, as they finished plastering here. We moved things in the rooms, and washed the floors, Nov. 7, 1913.

Nov. 13, 1913 – To-day it is very nice weather, a little foggy. We are going to Fred Arentsen's funeral, he died Nov. 10, in Council Bluffs.

June 25, 1913 – Martha Arentsen was buried to-day. It is very warm and nice. She died the 23 of June.

Page 13

Nov. 19, 1913 – We papered the dining room to-day, and cousin Martin [Christensen?][19] left for home to-day. He was here to say good-bye.

Nov. 20, 1913 – Ida and Mabel were over to our place last night. Mabel is getting a black dress made.

Nov. 30, 1913 – To-day is Sunday and it is very rainy. We are all alone home. We just got our new bureau and two dinning room chairs yesterday.

Dec. 5, 1913 – We were all over to P. Paulson's sale. It rained a little.

---

[19] Martin Christensen was eldest son of Lars Peter Christensen and Martine's sister, Minnie Nelson. The family lived in California by this time, but perhaps Martin was visiting or had stayed back until this time.

Dec. 15, 1913 – To-day is very nice weather D. Carmicael is over sawing wood to-day, and Andrews[20] were over too.

Dec. 31, 1913 – To-day is foggy and all the trees are white. Leo & Marie Weber were over here to-day and the Carlsons came also. We went to church in Harlan to watch meeting. There were 14 baptized. Rev. [Immanuel] Fredmund & his wife were there, they sang two or three songs. We stayed till after mid-night, we got home when it was 2 o'clock.

[20] Andrew is probably a first name. There are no Andrews surnames in the 1910 or 1920 census for either Monroe or Center township of Shelby County.

1914

Page 14

Jan 1, 1914 – To-day is a very windy day, Mamma & Mabel are down to Chipman's [21] to the Ladies Aid.

Jan. 18, 1914 – Yesterday was a very nice but was muddy. Oscar and I were to church both day and night, there were 21 baptized. Mabel had a bad cold so her & Mamma stayed home.

Jan. 28, 1914 – Mabel & Walter were married this evening. There were about 30 present. We had lap supper.

Feb. 3, 1914 – Oscar took Mabel & Walter to Harlan, They were going to Madelia Minn [22] and also to Clark's Grove [23].

Walter Larsen and Mabel Keldgord
(No photographer identified.)

---

[21] There is a Guy Chipman listed on Page 54 of the Sixtieth Anniversary of the Altamont Baptist Church of Cuppy's Grove, Harlan, Iowa as member.

[22] Walter's sister, Sine Jensen, lived in Madelia, Minnesota.

[23] Mabel's uncle Reverend Nels Nelson lived in Clarks Grove, Minnesota.

Feb. 6, 1914 – It is a very cold day to-day, it is snowing and drifting, Oscar just went to school, 10 o'clock.

Feb. 11, 1914 – We are going to town to-day. I am going to get a new Duck Coat. [Oscar?]

Feb. 24, 1914 – We sold 5 sows yesterday to Findlays and Walter hauled them in with our team. We got $8.10.

Page 15

Feb. 17, 1914 – To-day it is very nice weather, the snow is melting fast to-day, Oscar is sick & I guess he has the measles. We sold our 3 calves yesterday and they are gone to-day.

Feb. 24, 1914 – Geo Arentsen [24] died to-day, and will be buried the 26th at our church. 1 o'clock at the house, and 2 at the church.

March 5, 1914 – To-day is nice weather but it is a little cold. Oscar has been splitting wood, some of those big chunks. I have just gotten over the measles.

March 3, 1914 – Mabel & Walter moved into their house to-day. There is four rooms in their house.

March 13, 1914 – We were down to visit down in Walnut to-day, the first time to visit Mabel & Walter.

March 18, 1914 – We were to town to-day. It is a little cloudy and snowing a little. I got my new spring coat, $12.52. We visited Marinus C. in afternoon.

Page 16 Memorial

---

[24] George and Mary Arentsen had children: James, Martin, Stella, Elmer and Eddie listed in 1910 census. Mary was a sister to Minnie Christensen's husband.

March 20, 1914 – We got 53 eggs to-day. It is very nice weather.

March 22, 1914 – We were all to church to-day, it is very nice weather, the roads are fine. We went over to Peter Petersen's after church.

March 28, 1914 – It has been raining all night and some this forenoon. It is the biggest spring rain this year. The weather is getting clear and the grass is coming fast.

April 5, 1914 – I got my handkerchief & plate. Yesterday Mabel & Walter were home, and also Mabel & Clarence. It was a little chilly.

April 6, 1914 – To-day is quite nice weather, we washed, I also. We have one hen setting.

Easter April 12, 1914 – To-day we were to church, all but Mamma. The church was just full. Leo & Marie [Weber] & Swante [Kjeldgaard] [25] were here.

April 13, 1914 – To-day we planted our garden and flower garden and the 14th we papered the kitchen.

Page 17

I got my silver pocket book the first part in June. [written in top margin.]

May 13, 1914 – I came home to-day from working out by Chris M. Peterson's. I got $11.25.

May 15, 1914 – We were to town to-day to see the parade. I got my crepe dress and hand-bag yesterday.

---

[25] Svante Kjeldgaard was Anders Christian Svante Kjeldgaard, born in Granå, Denmark, April 16, 1893, son of Jacob's cousin Christian Andersen Kjeldgaard.

May 16 – A man is putting the screens on our new house to-day.

June 18, 1914 – Walter Findlay is plowing our corn the second time. Oscar & Mamma are in town to-day after a separator. We were over to Nels Chris[tensens?].

June 8, 1914 – We started to sell cream to Prairie Rose to-day.

June 10 – The strawberries are ripe now, and the cherries will soon be.

June 5 – We were to our school picnic over by center school & Vinnie Rold, Clarence Nelson, Esther Peterson graduated.

We had conference in our church from the 27 of May til the 1st of June, 1914.

Page 18

June 14, 1914 – To-day is Sunday. We are all home to-day because it is too muddy to go to church. In the afternoon, Car[s]ten & Pete Clausen & Nels Larsen[26] were up to see us.

June 17, 1914 – We are washing to-day. It is very nice weather. Our roses are in bloom and Findlays are thru plowing corn the second time. Swante & Pete Nelson [27] were up last night.

July 6, 1914 – To-day it is raining and we were out picking rasp-berries this morning. We are about thru picking them. We have sold 24 quts at 25¢ a quart.

July 4, 1914 – We were all out to the grove to-day. Mabel & Walter came home last night. We had a pretty good time. They had 2 stands, ice cream & plums, candy, etc. to sell.

---

[26] Nels Larsen was Walter's father.
[27] Pete Nelson may have been Martine's brother.

Page 19

July 5, 1914 - To-day we had a very enjoyable day. We had company from Omaha, our 2nd cousins, Cathrine, Cristine and Clara Kjeldgaard. Svante [Kjeldgaard] [28] was also up. We had our pictures taken many times. Hans Rasmussens were up in the after-noon.

Kathrine, Clara & Christine Kjeldgaard (family photo)

July 20, 1914 – We started to pick black-berries to-day and to the 25th of July we have picked 83qts.

July 13 – I started to work over by cousin Marie[29] & Leo [Weber] to-day and stayed till the 22nd of July.

---

[28] These were daughters of Christen Andersen Kjeldgaard who were all born in Nebraska. Christen and Svante's father, Christian, were brothers, and both were cousins to Jacob Keldgord.
[29] Cousin Marie was Marie M. Nielsen, daughter of Pete and Zena Nielsen, "Iowa, Marriages, 1809-1992," index, FamilySearch

Aug. 2, 1914 – We have picked 160 qt of black-berries. We were to the show last night. And I and Mrs. Berg and children are alone home to-day, Mamma and Oscar went to church.

Aug. 4, 1914 – To-day Mrs. Berg & kids and Stella [30] & kids are staying here. It is Stella's birthday she is 27 yrs. old [31]. Velma is 5 yrs & Maxine is 7 yrs.

Page 20

Aug. 11, 1914 – We were to church to-day. It is very hot & dusty. Their were lots of people in church. I went to church in the evening, M.E. church. We picked 175 quarts of black-berries this year. We had quite a few yellow crabs too.

Aug. 9, 1914 – To-day we are alone home, but had company for dinner. Mr. and Mrs. Chris Petersen & Babe were here from Jacksonville.

Aug 19, 1914 – To-day we have picked wild grapes, and Oscar & I were in town this forenoon. We are going to get a phone put in, in a couple of days. Nels Christensens are threshing to-day.

Aug. 20, 1914 – We got our phone put in this morning. Two men were out to put it in.

Aug. 24, 1914 – Fair starts to-day.

(https://familysearch.org/pal:/MM9.1.1/XJW1-4JV : accessed 29 Dec 2013), Leo A. Weber and Marie M. Nielsen, 29 Oct 1912.
[30] Stella is Stella Keldgord Plummer, a cousin to Martha and daughter of Chris Keldgord. Chris was a brother and neighbor to Jacob. Stella married Joe Plummer, living in Nebraska and Mason City, Iowa.
[31] Stella Keldgord of Center Twp, Shelby County was born in August 1887 according to the 1900 census confirming her 27th birthday in August 1914.

Aug. 23, 1914 – We were home to-day. It is Sunday. Swante, Alvin Christensen & a little boy from Council Bluffs were here for dinner. Mabel Berg was also here and stayed all day.

Page 21 Memorandum

Aug. 26, 1914 – To-day we have been to Fair in Harlan. We had a pretty good time. It was quite nice weather but awful dusty. I stayed for the Chase Lister show in the evening. Anthon & Grace were with us, we were out auto riding.

Aug. 27, 1914 – To-day it is raining and is chilly. It is the last day of the fair.

Aug. 30, 1914 – We went all down to Walnut to visit. We got home about 8 o'clock in the evening. Walter's mother is in Minn now.

Sept. 4, 1914 J. M. Jensen's has a baby girl born the 4th in Minnesota.[32] I got my winter blue hat the 4th.

Sept. 12, 1914 – We have been in town to-day. It was a little cold and windy. We stopped at Paulson's a little while.

Sept. 13 – We are going out to Harvest feast at our church to-day. There were about 300 people. We were also their in the evening. [Rev.] W. [J.] Andresen was the speaker.

Page 22

Sept. 22, 1914 – I got my suede slippers to-day. We were all in town yesterday, to funeral, old man Bisgaard was buried.[33]

---

[32] Walter's sister was Jensine Martine Jensen who lived in Madelia, Minnesota. This daughter was Ida Marie Jensen.
[33] A Christian J. Bisgaard, 1839 – 1914, was buried in the Harlan Cemetery. (Find A Grave Memorial# 38541186)

Sept. 23, 1914 – To-day is a very nice day and autumn starts also. Oscar is in school to-day. Anna Carlson is starting to sew my blue shally wool dress this week.

Oct. 1, 1914 – To-day is Mamma's birthday. She is 53 years old. She got a berry spoon. We had the Ladies Aid Society meet at our house to-day. Their were quite a few people here.

Oct. 8, 1914 - To-day we came home from Omaha after being their since Sunday, Oct. 4. We was in for the Ak-sar-ben [34] and the electric parade. We had a very good time. We came to Harlan at noon, and went to the Farmers Institute in the afternoon.

Oct. 9, 1914 – To-day it is rainy weather and we are very busy cleaning up. Oscar got his new suit yesterday.

Page 23

Oct. 17, 1914 - To-day is a very pretty day, the sun is very warm. The people going to pick corn soon.

Oct. 20, 1914 – We have been to town to-day, it was very nice weather. Oscar got his new Elgin watch to-day $5.50 and I got my pink auto scarf. Mr. & Mrs. Christensen were up here to-day. We sold over 14 bu. old corn 53¢ a bu.

Oct. 18, 1914 – We were all down to see Mabel & Walter Sunday.

Oct. 25, 1914 – To-day it is a little cold it frost last night for the first time this fall. We are going to church to-day.

Oct. 27, 1914 – To-day is a very nice day. We got our cows in the stalks. Walter F. [Findlay] is over picking corn here to-day.

---

[34] The Ak-Sar-Ben horse track was not built until 1920. This probably refers to the Ak-Sar-Ben Den which hosted various performances along with the electric parade.

Nov. 1, 1914 – To-day it is very nice weather, Svante & I went down to Walnut. I stayed until the 5th.

Page 24 Memoriam

Nov. 22, 1914 – To-day it is real nice weather but a little cold. We were over to Leo & Marie's for dinner. Chris Hesses were down to. In the evening we went to church, they had a mission program. It was very good.

Nov. 26, 1914 – Martha & Magnus [35] were married to-day. To-day is Thanksgiving day, we are alone home it is very nice weather.

Dec. 1, 1914 – To-day is a very nice day. Oscar went to school to-day. Yesterday was very foggy and it rained last night.

Dec. 10, 1914 – To-day is pretty cold and frosty, and snow on the ground, we were over to Marie's club, there were quite a few there and we had a good time.

Dec. 12, 1914 – To-day a baby boy [Melvin] was born to Mr. & Mrs. Walter Larsen. We went down their in the afternoon and I stai'd down there 3 weeks and now I am home I came home Jan. 2, 1915.

Page 25

Dec. 24, 1914 – Mamma and Oscar were over to Nels Christensen's to eat Christmas eve supper.

Dec. 31, 1914 – To-day Oscar was in town to bring our new base burner out home.

---

[35] Probably Magnus Jensen. There was a Magnus and Martha Jensen nearby.

Martha Keldgord's Journal 1911 - 1930

1915

Jan. 5, 1915 – To-day is very muddy and wet weather. It has melted almost all the snow off the ground. The wind is in the south.

1915 – May all happiness be your this year and may this gladness be renewed each coming year.

Just a little wish on this little card. It's simple happy days but I wish it awful hard. [signed] Clarence Keldgord [36] Jan. 11, 1915.

Jan. 11, 1915 – To-day we were in after Clarence & his mother. They stayed over night and we took them in the next day.

Page 26 Memoriam

Jan. 10, 1915 – Mabel Berg came out to-night with somebody [Looks like "(H.G.)" was squeezed in.] and stayed till the 12th when we took her in. It was very muddy and cold.

Jan. 3, 1915 – To-day I got my signat ring for Xmas.

Dec. 1915 [1915 is written in ink rather than the pencil used for the rest of the page. It probably should be Dec. 1914.] – I got a broach for Xmas, a hand painted plate, a brown sweater and barrett.

---

[36] Clarence Keldgord, along with Stella and Elmer, were Martha's cousins. They were children of Chris Keldgord. Their parents were divorced and Chris had died. They lived in Omaha with their mother, Christine.

Jan. 16, 1915 – To-day it is snowing and drifting, and Oscar is in town with some corn to feed Findlay's hogs with. They hauled 12 loads. I am going to iron to-day.

Jan. 19, 1915 – To-day it is snowing and drifting, and Oscar is in town with some corn to feed Findlay's hogs with. They hauled 12 loads. I am going to iron to-day.

Jan. 21, 1915 – To-day it is freezing pretty hard, it is snowing a little all the time. We got in 6 eggs.

Feb. 11, 1915 – To-day it has been melting but real nice weather. I was over the club [37] at Nels Christensen's. I got an apron.

Page 27 Memoriam

Feb. 17, 1915 – To-day it has been very dark cloudy, and is raining to-night while we were doing chores. Mabel & Walter are down to Bisgaard's, Walt is helping W. B.[Willads Bisgaard][38] haul machinery to Walnut. I made my new corset cover to-day and finished my pin cushion last night. The roads are very bad. [In the margin was the following:] We got in 9 eggs.

Feb. 24, 1915 – We got 24 eggs to-day. We washed and ironed also.

---

[37] This possibly referred to the Center Country Club, a group of women from Center Township who met to "improve the conditions of life surrounding the women of country homes" according to Edward S, White, The Past and Present of Shelby County, Volume 2, page 467, 1915.
[38] Walter's brother-in-law was Willads Bisgaard.

Feb. 24, 1915 – To-day is very nice weather, the sun is shining, nice and warm. Anna Carlson & Earl McDonald were married at Evergreen Hill [39] at 2 o'clock.

Feb. 27, 1915 – We got in 30 eggs. We were all to town to-day, the weather was cloudy and cold. I got my silver thimble and my table scarf.

Mar. 3, 1915 – To-day Mrs. [Willads] Bisgaard and children left on the 11:18 train for Emmetsburg, Iowa.

Mar. 4, 1915 – To-day it is snowing all day, and the wind is blowing. We got in 38 eggs.

Page 28

March 11, 1915 – To-day it is real nice weather. I was to club down by Sena Hansen.

March 12, 1915 – Mr. S. Carlson died to-day at Des Moines Lutheran Hospital. He was operated upon the 10th. The funeral will be held Monday the 15th. The boys will be pall bearers.

T. R. Nelson's mother died 20th. [between entries]

March 22, 1915 – To-day it is nice weather. Ma & Oscar went to town, and also to Soren Miller's funeral. He died the 19th.

April 1, 1915 – To-day it is real nice weather. We went down to Walnut to visit Mabel. We were down to Walter's mother and was up town a little while to. We went 8 o'clock and come back 7 o'clock.

April 4, 1915 – To-day it has been real nice weather. We went to church & Sunday school. In the evening a few young people

---

[39] The 1911 Atlas of Shelby County Iowa shows that the school just west of Keldgord's was called Evergreen Hill.

were invited to come and help me celebrate my 20th birthday. We had a very good time. I rec'd 4 presents and 4 cards. They staid until a late hour. 2 plates & 2 handerkerchiefs, handbag, & thimble.

Page 29 Memorial

April 6, 1915 – We have been raking the yard and having bonfires to-day. Planted garden. We got 72 eggs to-day. We have 2 hens setting.

April 10, 1915 – Pete Paulson died to-day in Harlan.

April 11, 1915 – To-day it is very nice weather. We went all to church, and Sunday school, and to Pete Petersen after church.

April 14, 1915 – To-day it has been very warm weather. I Kalsomined the little bedroom and painted the woodwork. In the evening we went up to Soren Jensen's.

April 15, 1915 – We got in 98 eggs to-night. It has been very warm. We varnished the front room and Mamma's bedroom & put the carpet down.

April 18, 1915 – To-day it is real nice weather. It is very warm. Mabel came home and is going to stay home for a while. Jim [40] and Walter and Grandma & Grandpa [41] came also along up. We went to town in the afternoon, some of us, and in the evening we went all to the Harlan Danish Church to the silver wedding.

Page 30

April 25, 1915 – It is real nice weather. We were to church in the forenoon. Mabel & her baby went along with us.

---

[40] This is probably Walter Larsen's brother Jens, known as Jim.
[41] Grandma and Grandpa may refer to Walter and Jim's parents, Nels Peter and Beathe Larsen.

April 30, 1915 – It is a little cloudy to-day, but not very warm. We planted trees yesterday & the lilac bush. Oscar & I were in town in the forenoon. I had poison on my arms and face, the doctor gave me something to put on them. We have 5 little pigs & 23 little chickens. We got 10 hens setting. Leo & Marie were over here to-night.

May 2, 1915 – To-day we have been alone home all day. It has been raining nearly all day. They had their church dedicated (Lutherans) to-day. Oscar got his bicycle yesterday.

May 16, 1915 – To-day is Sunday. It is blowing pretty hard and is chilly too. We did not go to church. In the afternoon Leo & Marie & Bernice [Weber] & Grace were over. In the evening Leo took us to church. [Rev.]W. [J.] Andreasen was there.

Page 31

May 18, 1915 – We are washing to-day. It is quite windy. Oscar took in 3 of our sows to-day. He went with Martin Arentsen. We have about 60 little chickens and quite a few hens setting. 8 little pigs [in margin]. To-night P[eter] C. Larsen is going to preach his farewell sermon. He is going to S. D. [At top of page]

May 27, 1915 – To-day it is very rainy and cold. Mrs. Holmes is sewing my dresses and also Anna A.'s dress. We have over 100 chickens.

June 6, 1915 – To-day we went to church & Sunday school, and we went down to Geo Arentsen's for dinner.

June 9, 1915 – To-day Leo, Marie [Weber], Martha & Bernice & Edna Mae went to Denison. We got up 4 o'clock and started half past 5. We got up there at 7 o'clock. We were up for carnival and sure had a good time. We staid over night and came back the next day.

[signed Kelgord, not Keldgord] Martha P. Kelgord. June 11, 15 Age 20.

Page 32 Memorial

June 17, 1915 – To-day it has rained nearly all day. Oscar went to town this afternoon after our lawn swing and staid in town during the storm. Our roses are starting to bloom.

June 13, 1915 – To-day Mabel & Walter & baby were home. We went all to church to-day. It was children's day.

June 27, 1915 - To-day Leo & Marie took us down to Walnut. We had a very good time. The roads were very good.

July 3, 1915 – The people in Kirkman celebrated the 4th. It wasn't a very nice day.

July 4, 1915 – To-day it is a very nice day although the roads are a little damp. We were home all day, but to-night we are all going out to the church to hear Esther Christensen who is going to speak.

July 11, 1915 – To-day it is very nice weather. Oscar & I went to church & Sunday School. In the evening it rained very hard and thundered and lightning. The nastuturms [nasturtiums?] & pansies blooming.

Page 33 Memorial

July 15, 1915 – To-day it is a very warm day. Findlays are making hay over here. We had a big rain over here to-night, almost a cloud burst.

July 18, 1915 – Yesterday Mabel & Melvin came home. To-day we were to have the young folks rally at Cuppy's Grove but it rained nearly all day. It was real nice in the evening.

July 20, 1915 - To-day it is very nice weather. We ironed to-day and went in to Stena Sahl's for dinner, and went up town after dinner.

July 21, 1915 – To-day Mrs. Sahl & Mrs. Madson are going to leave for a trip out west to Wash & Calif.

Aug. 1, 1915 – To-day Mabel & Melvin & I and Oscar went to church. It looked like rain in the afternoon, it did not rain up here but in Walnut it did.

Aug. 4, 1915 – To-night Jim is coming after Mabel and Melvin spending 2 wks and a half with us. We had Melvin's picture taken on a postal the first time, it was very good of him.

Page 34 – Memorandum

Aug. 7, 1915 – To-day Oscar is helping Leo's make hay. They finished to-day all but a load & half. Mamma & I drove alone to-day. I got Lavaliere [pendant] from Mamma.

Aug. 14, 1915 – To-day Old Chris Christensen [42]died. Will be buried Monday.

Aug. 15, 1915 – To-day we are alone home. We are going out to church to-night to hear Ralph Jensen who is going to preach.

Aug. 23, 1915 – Yesterday Svante & I were in Walnut. We went down Saturday night and came back Sunday night. Fair starts to-day. We are going in Wednesday.

Aug. 24, 1915 – To-day we were to fair in the afternoon and I stayed for fireworks in the evening. And the 25th we were all in there all day and sure had a fine time. Oscar & I went in for the Chase-Lister in the evening.

---

[42] C. B. Christiansen 1835 – 1915 was buried at Cuppy's Grove according to Find-A-Grave Memorial # 98315048.

Aug. 20, 1915 – Mrs. Pete Peterson was operated on to-day for appendicitis in Omaha. She will come home the 29th.

Sept. 5, 1915 – To-day is real nice weather. Yesterday we were in town. I got my winter hat. I think we will go to church to-day.

Page 35

Sept 3, 1915 – We were to a social to-day over by Nels Christensen's . It started at four o'clock in the afternoon and lasted thru'out the evening.

Sept. 5, 1915 – To-day the weather is very nice. We were to church, and Backs were here for dinner, and in the afternoon Hans Rassmusens were up here & also Niel Berg.

Sept. 15, 1915 – To-day we started about 8 o'clock for Walnut, and was down there about 10 o'clock. And after dinner we went down to Walter folks and then it started to rain, so we start home about 4 o'clock.

Sept. 12, 1915 – We were to tent meeting in the afternoon and I stayed in for the evening. [Rev.] P. C. Nelson & Garmong [Rev.Christen P. Grarup?] and Rev. [E. H.?] & Mrs. Clark are with the tent.

Sept. 18, 1915 – To-day the weather is very nice. We went to town in the afternoon and Mamma got her glasses and I started my [bracelet?].

Page 36 Memorandum

Sept. 19, 1915 – We were all to church to-day. P. C. Nelson was to our church and spoke this forenoon. This afternoon he is to speak in Harlan on the subject "If Christ came to Harlan" and he is going to speak on the subject "A kiss in the dark and what came of it." We are all going in to-night.

Oct. 6, 1915 – To-day it is a little chilly [and it was?] the first day of the Farmer's Institute. Yesterday we were to the funeral of Lester Smith. He died Sunday. Ma & I got our new blue woolen dress goods, and Oscar got his overcoat.

Oct. 24, 1915 – To-day it is very nice weather. Mabel & Walter & Melvin was here, Leo & Marie [Weber] & Bernice were her for dinner. Mabel & Walter went to church in the forenoon. We all went out auto riding in the afternoon.

Oct. 29, 1915 – To-day we are cleaning house. We cleaned all but the kitchen & north room.

Page 37

Oct. 28, 1915 – To-day it is very nice weather. We went out to see Mr. & Mrs. Carl McDonald. We had dinner and staid thru the afternoon and had a very good time.

Oct. 20 - Mrs. Wilson is here now and is making our blue woolen dresses.

Oct. 30, 1915 – To-day it is very nice weather. Mabel & Walter & Melvin came home. Leo & Marie & Bernice [Weber] were also her. We went out auto ride in the afternoon.

Nov. 7, 1915 – To-day it is very windy. We went to church and there were 7 baptized. It rained when we went home from church.

Nov. 8, 1915 – To-day we put our cattle in the stalks and we put them in the barn the first time this fall.

Nov. 19, 1915 – To-day the wind is blowing hard and is very cold. Mamma and Oscar went to town. Oscar had two teeth filled. We got our new lap robe.

Page 38 Memorandum

Nov. 25, 1915 – To-day is Thanksgiving and Pete Peterson's were here for dinner. In the evening Svante and I went to Omaha on the 7:35. We had a very good time. Clara and I went to Riverview Park [43] Friday. We came home Sunday evening.

Dec. 9, 1915 – To-day I took our hogs to town and they weighed 975. We got $58.50. [Oscar]

Dec. 12, 1915 – We bought 6 little pigs of Leo to-day. [added between entries.]

Dec. 5, 1915 – To-day we were to church and came home about 2:30 and ate our dinner and done the chores. We went to Harlan church in the evening.

Dec. 11, 1915 – To-day we went to town. The ground was covered with snow. There were many people in town.

Dec. 12, 1915 – To-day Mamma, Oscar & I were over to Leo's [Weber] for dinner and Bernice had the measles. It is Melvin's Birthday. He is 1 yr old. We talked to Mabel over the phone.

Page 39

Dec. 22, 1915 – To-day is a very nice day. John Rold sawed wood for us. Martin and Harold helped saw.

Dec. 23, 1915 – Svante [Kjeldgaard] was here after he quit his work in town. He left for Omaha the 24th to spend Xmas.

Dec. 24 – Mabel and Walter & Melvin came home on the 2 o'clock, and in the afternoon, Oscar and I went up to the school house to hear the program and see the Christmas tree. In the

---

[43] Riverview Park was a scenic park in Omaha, featuring wild deer and buffalo. The zoo would eventually be located there.

evening we went to see the Xmas trees in town, in the court house lawns and in the Danish Church.

Dec. 25, 1915 – To-day it is fair weather. Bergs were all here for dinner and we had a very good time.

For Xmas I got a manicure set, a hair receiver, gloves, stationary, hat pin, calendar, pin cushion, and got my friendship bracelet finished, a Turkish towel, a book "Polly a New Fashioned Girl", two little plates.

Page 40 Memorandum

Dec. 29, 1915 – To-day the weather is fair. Walter, Mabel, Melvin, Oscar & I went over to Leo's for dinner.

This month I learned to crochet.

Dec. 31, 1915 – To-day it has rained nearly all day. It has been foggy. It is so slippery outside. To-day I sewed two waists and an apron. Oscar & I have got a bad cold.

Martha Keldgord's Journal 1911 - 1930

1916

Jan. 2, 1916 – To-day it is very nice weather but a little muddy. Oscar and I went to church. P.C. was here in the afternoon. [above this entry was the following:] Johanna Jensen [44] died the 3rd or 4th [It looks like "3rd or" was crossed out leaving the 4th.], will be buried the 6th.

Jan. 6, 1916 – To-day Walter, Oscar & I went to town to the funeral. Johanna Jensen was buried. There were lots of flowers. I got my new lace patented leather shoes to-day.

Jan. 7, 1916 – To-day Mabel & Walter & Melvin left on the 9:18 for Ruthven. They went to visit Bisgaards.

Jan. 10, 1916 – To-day the wind is in the northwest, it is quite cold. I have been sick with the grip the last 3 days.

Jan. 11 – It is snowing to-day.

Page 41 Memorandum

Jan. 12, 1916 – To-day it is very cold and snowing and drifting hard too. We can't hardly keep warm in the house. 28° below. We got 10 eggs [yesterday?].

Jan. 23, 1916 – To-day the weather has been nice, but it has melted and the snow is almost gone. We were all alone home all day.

Jan. 25, 1916 – To-day the weather has been cold and the ground is almost covered with snow as it has snowed all day. Harold

[44] Johannah M. Jensen 1900 – 1916 was buried in the Harlan Cemetery according to Find-A-Grave Memorial # 38789079.

Findlay is sick in bed. He has been in bed a week and they have a nurse to take care of him. He has plurisy.

Feb. 1, 1916 – I came home from Leo's to-day after staying there a few days helping them pack. They took their furniture and things to town to-day. They left for Denison to-day. Feb. 3, 1916. Oscar and I took them to town.

Page 42 Memorandum

Feb. 4, 1916 – To-night we went to Sam Michaelson's to bible study. Martin and Anna went with us.

Feb. 5, 1916 – To-day we were in town in the bob-sled. It is very good roads for sleighing now. There were quite a few people in town.

Feb. 21, 1916 – To-day the weather is very nice. It is melting, the snow is almost gone. We was over to Nels Christensen's this afternoon. I was crocheting on my corset cover yoke.

Feb. 22, 1916 – To-day the weather is damp and foggy. Harry Hansen was up here and blasted those big logs.

Feb. 26, 1916 – To-day it is blowing and snowing. It is quite cold. Mabel & Clarence and Harry were over to-night. We sang and played on the organ and had a good time. Oscar got 4 neck ties and gloves and kakis. [45]

Page 43

Feb. 28, 1916 – To-day it was snowing early this morning but it cleared up and 9 'oclock we started for Walnut. We got down there about half past 11. We got home about 7 o'clock. I got my ring with three sets in it.

---

[45] Oscar Keldgord was born February 26, 1900, making this his 16th birthday.

March 1, 1916 – To-day it is snowing and the roads are rough. Hans Carlson's moved to-day about 2 [H...?]. Martin and Anna and Harry were up last night.

March 5, 1916 – To-day it is real nice weather. We went to church and Sunday school. In the evening we went down to Hansen's.

March 7, 1916 – It is blowing very hard and is cold. We went to funeral, Mrs. Thompson died the 4th and was buried the 7th. There was quite a few people there. [Between entries is the following:] Martin and Vina was married the 22nd.

March 25, 1916 – Last night we was over by Anna and Eddie. Martin & Vina [Arentsen] came home last night from Council Bluffs on their wed trip.

Page 44

April 4, 1916 – To-day the weather is real nice but a little cold. We went to town. I got my blue silk poplin goods.

April 5, 1916 – Ida Sahl made my dress to-day.

April 7, 1916 – To-day it is cold and it is snowing a little.

April 10, 1916 – To-day is very warm and nice weather. We washed, and planted the garden to-day.

April 12, 1916 – We have only 4 hens setting. We have cleaned the kitchen and pantry.

April 13, 1916 – To-day it is a little cloudy and rainy. We were out by R. J. Rassmusen's to Golden Wedding They served a four-course cold supper. The Danish church gave them 50 roses for a remembrance. They got quite a few presents.

April 23, 1916 – To-day it is a little cloudy and cold. We were in church. We went down to Arentsen's [46] for dinner. There were quite a few in church.

Page 45

May 7, 1916 – We were home all day to-day (Sun). R. J. Rassmusens were all here for dinner and Carsten Clausen was here in the afternoon.

May 17, 1916 – To-day the weather is real nice, we [washed?] out by Rassmusen's. They all went along home when they bro't me out here.

June 4, 1916 - To-day we are alone home all day. Mabel and Melvin came home Friday night. We went to picnic Friday. Mabel [Christensen] went with us over there. There were 11 graduates, 6 from our school. It was conference Sunday in Merrill's Grove There were 1000 people out there on Sunday and 157 autos. [In the margin was written:] We started to sell cream the 6th 34¢ a lb.

June 5, 1916 – Mrs. Alex Samuels [47] died this afternoon and was buried the 7th. There was a big crowd out there, 85 autos. They had so many pretty flowers.

Page 46

June 16, 1916 - To-day we went all out to Jacksonville, Mabel & Melvin were along out there. The weather was nice. Their peonies were in bloom.

---

[46] Arentsen's lived one mile south of Cuppy's Grove.
[47] Katherine Elizabeth Samuels, 1849 – 1916, was buried at Cuppy's Grove according to Find-A-Grave Memorial # 62008101.

June 18, 1916 – To-day it rained a little in the morning but it soon cleared off again. Oscar & I went to church for children's program. Mabel and I went to church for children's day program. Mabel and Melvin went home in the evening. They from Walnut went to the convention in the afternoon and evening, we had the baby at home.

July 1, 1916 – To-day it is very warm, one of the hottest days we have had this summer. We stayed home all day and went to church in the evening to hear Dr. Lapham of Des Moines.

July 4, 1916 – To-day it rained in the forenoon, in the afternoon it cleared off. We went with Louis in his car to town. I came with A. S. home.

Page 47

July 5, 1916 – To-day we picked 18 quts of raspberries. We sold them at 15¢.

July 8, 1916 – I got my white buckskin skippers.

July 12, 1916 – To-day we finished picking raspberries. We have picked 60 qut. Oscar is helping Roy haul hogs to-day. We are going to get Mrs. Wilson to-day. She is going to make our flowered dresses.

July 16, 1916 – To-day the weather was real nice. They had the BYPU [48] rally in Harlan. We went in the evening.

Aug. 10, 1916 – To-day it is real nice weather. Oscar and I were over to Klints for club, and in the evening we all went out to ice-cream social. Mabel and Melvin were along out there. It was nice moonlight and there was a big crowd.

---

[48] BYPU is short for the Baptist Young People's Union.

Aug. 11, 1916 – To-day we have picked 10 quts and altogether 181 quts we sold.

Page 48

Aug. 24, 1916 – To-day it is very nice weather. Rudolf Klints threshed to-day and came over and started to thresh here at 6 o'clock and got thru half past 7.

Aug. 21, 1916 – To-day the weather is nice. Oscar and I went to the fair all day and we went wed. the 23rd to see the fireworks, they were fine.

Sept. 10, 1916 – To-day I am out by R. J. Rasmussen's. It is a little cloudy and rainy. We had meeting at 3 o'clock and there were quite a few people from Harlan Danish Church.

Sept. 17, 1916 – To-day it is very nice weather. We went to Correction Grove to the forenoon meeting and went to Fiscus in the afternoon meeting to hear [Rev.] W. [J.] Andreasen and Ras took me out home in the evening. We rode 50 miles in the Apperson that day.

Page 49

Sept. 24, 1916 – To-day the weather is very nice. We were at home all day. Lewis was up in the afternoon and Peter Clausen and Sena Damguard were up to see us in the evening.

Sept. 18, 1916 – Ida Sahl came to sew for us to-day. She made Mamma's gray silk dress and mine and Mabel's silk waists.

Oct. 1, 1916 – To-day the weather is awfully windy and Mabel & Walter & Melvin were home. It was Mamma's birthday. In the afternoon Sahl's bro't Stena up here a little while.

Oct. 15, 1916 – To-day we had "Young People's Rally" at our church. It was a little rainy in the forenoon but was quite nice in the afternoon. There were quite a few people there. We had lunch at noon. We were also out there a little while in the afternoon. Dr. Wilcox spoke in the evening.

Oscar was in Omaha 26th and 27th. Oscar saw Wilson and the electric parade at Omaha. [written between entries and in margin.]

Page 50

Oct. 19, 1916 -To-day it started to mist and finally turned to sleet and then snow. It snowed all afternoon and took the cows in the barn that night. And to-day the 20th it is very cold. It also froze hard. The snow is about 6 in. dp.

Oct. 26, 1916 – To-day Oscar & I went to town in the forenoon and I went over to help Mabel [Christensen] celebrate her birthday. 21 years old. Mrs. Chris Hansen also.

Oct. 27, 1916 – To-day the weather is just fine. Oscar went in after Truelson. He papered our dining room, striped paper. We took him back home in the evening.

Nov. 1, 1916 – To-day the weather is just fine. We went down to see Mabel & Walter & baby. We went up town in the afternoon and then down to Grandma [Larsen?]'s.

Page 51

Oct. 31 & Nov. 2 – I went down to Roy's to help Minnie clean house, the upstairs & bedroom, front room & dining room.

Nov. 7, 1916 – Yesterday we were in town in the lumber wagon. Oscar sold his bicycle to Richard Kemp for $8.00. [Oscar bought it May 2, 1915.] Last night we were over by Martin and Vina

[Arentsen] . To-day it is raining. We have started to rake the yard.

Nov. 5th - Pete & Lewis were here for dinner last Sunday. We went to Walnut in the afternoon.

Nov. 11, 1916 – It is snowing a little to-day. We put up our hard coal stove. Findlays got thru picking corn to-day.

Nov. 12, 1916 – To-day it is snowing. Martin and Vin & Martin M. & Louis' were over for dinner.

Nov. 13, 1916 – Carsten Tobiason [49] died the 11th of Nov. and was buried to-day the 13th. There was a big funeral.

Page 52

Nov. 9, 1916 – John Sorensen and Marie Simmonsen were married to-day. They were married at Hans Bensons'.

Nov. 19, 1916 – To-day the weather just like spring. Oscar and I went to church & Sunday school. Pete Petersen's were with us home for dinner and in the afternoon Soren Jensen's & Fred Carlson's were up to visit us.

Nov. 21, 1916 – To-day it is dark and cloudy. Oscar took 5 of our biggest spring pigs. They weighed 192 a piece at 9¢ a lb.

Nov. 25, 1916 – To-day the weather is fine. Andrew Nelson started to build our new hog house. It is 30 x 20 and 10 bins in it.

Nov. 25 – Oscar and I went down to Chris Hansen's sale. Everything sold well. Pigs sold from $22 to $26, weight lbs. Cows sold from $92 to $170. Weather was just fine. Lots of people there.

---

[49] Carsten Tobiesen, 1840 – Nov. 11, 1916, was buried at Cuppy's Grove according to Find-A-Grave Memorial # 98323246.

Page 53

Nov. 30, 1916 – To-day the weather is just fine. It is Thanksgiving Day. There is meeting out in Merrill's Grove Church to-day. Cuppy's Grove and Harlan Danish church is invited. We are all alone home all day.

Dec. 7, 1916 – To-day Andrew Nelson finished our hog house.

Dec. 10, 1916 – To-day we were down to Walnut, it was cloudy all day.

Dec. 22, 1916 – To-day Oscar took 3 of our pigs to-day. We got $9.40 of Muldoon. In the afternoon we went up to the school house to see a Xmas tree and also a program. Myrtle Byers was teacher.

Dec. 24, 1916 – To-day the weather is real nice. Bergs were all out here for dinner and lunch. Mabel had just come back from Chicago [50]. Mabel & Walter & Melvin is coming home next Tuesday the 26th.

Page 54 Memorandum

Dec. 25, 1916 - To-day the weather has been cloudy and windy. To-night it thundered and lightninged, and rained a little. We were home all day.

Dec. 26, 1916 – To-day we went in after Mabel & Walter. They came on the Rock Island.

Dec. 31, 1916 – Oscar & Walter went to church to-day. It snowed nearly all day. We went with Louis to Harlan church, all of us but Ma & Melvin. They had watch meeting. Oscar got sick

---

[50] Martine's brother, Nels Nelson, was living in Chicago at the time.

to-night. A touch of appendicitis. We had the docter Monday
night.

1917

Jan. 5, 1917 – Louis took I & Mabel & Walter to town. We had Melvin's picture taken sitting on a little chair.

Jan. 6, 1917 – Mabel & Walter & I are going to church to-morrow. There is going to be baptism. 8 of them were baptized. We went down to Arentsen's for dinner.

Page 55 Memorandum

Jan. 14, 1917 – To-day the weather is cold, and frosty. Oscar & I and Mabel & Walter & Melvin were in church. We were down to Jim Andersen's for dinner.

Jan. 15, 1917 – To-day Jim came up after Mabel & Walter after staying here 3 wks. It is snowing a little.

I finished my square corset cover yoke last week the 12th.

Jan. 20, 1917 - To-day the weather is fair, Rudy butchered our pig.

Jan. 21, 1917 – To-day it is blowing, snowing & raining. We are alone home all day.

Jan. 24, 1917 – To-day the weather is fine. Hannah Rassmussen & Charlie Lansman were married at Hans Jensen's south of Harlan.

Jan. 25, 1917 – To-day the weather is nice. We went over to Sam Mickelsen's in bobsled.

Page 56

Jan. 22, 1917 – Miss Johanna Larsen was married to Mr. Carl Larsen Oct. 19, 1916 at McCook Nebr.

Jan. 27, 1917 – To-day it is fine weather. Oscar & Mamma went to town. Mrs. Nels Christensen has been in Omaha trading. She bo't my black silk poplin skirt & crepe decking waist. All of Nels Christensens were over for supper. Mabel [Christensen] got her waist just like mine.

Jan. 28, 1917 – To-day the weather is real nice, but it is muddy. We were up by Soren Jensen's & Fred Carlsons were staying up there. Pete Clausen was up there too.

Jan. 31, 1917 – To-day it is snowing and blowing. It is awful cold also. Our cows were in the barn nearly all day. We got in 6 eggs.

Feb. 1, 1917 – To-day it is very cold. It is 25 below zero. We have to sit close by the stove to keep warm.

Page 57

Feb. 4, 1917 – To-day it is a blizzard. It is pretty cold too, the wind is blowing and it is drifting hard. 14 below.

Feb. 7, 1917 – To-day it is real nice weather. The snow is melting off. Oscar & I were up to Soren Jensen and Carlson's to-day. I crochet that big doily pattern off, and Oscar bought a disc for $10.00.

Feb. 18, 1917 - To-day it is fair weather. Oscar & I went to church in forenoon & Louis took us to church in the evening. We got in 15 eggs again.

Feb. 20, 1917 – To-day we got in 21 eggs. It is real nice weather.

Feb. 21, 1917 – To-day the weather is real nice. There is a little snow on the ground. Rudolph Klindts are going to move 1st of March. He was over here to-day. Forest F. [Findlay] rented the north 40 to-day. We bought our Ford to-day of Booth. $392.

Page 58

Feb. 24, 1917 – We drove our new car to town to-day. Oscar learned to run the car to-day and Oscar & I drove it out alone to-night.

Mar. 1, 1917 – To-day Oscar & I took Andrew Nelson in to town. He finished building the piece to our auto shed.

Mar. 3, 1917 –To-day it is a little chilly. We went to town in our Ford. The roads are fine. I got my new tan & green plaid spring coat. $12.00.

Mar. 9, 1917 – To-day the weather is just like spring. We were to town in our car. We had the side curtains on. The roads are fine. We visited Stena Sahl, Old Andrew, & Trena Fredricksens & Mrs. Holmes was there and then we went up around Martin & Vina's place. We visited them the first time on George Therkelsen's place.

Mar. 7, 1917 – Anna Christensen & Ed Andersen was married to-day at Des Moines by Pro. S[oren] P. Fogdall.

Page 59

Mar. 11, 1917 – To-day the weather is real nice, but it is a little cloudy. We are home to-day. Pete Clausen & Andrew Sorensen came out here in the afternoon. Louis & Oscar & I went to church in our car up to Martin's place. Went in Louis' car to church at night.

Mar. 13, 1917 – The weather is very wet & dark to-day. It is sleeting & snowing very hard to-day, Martin & Louis came up here a little while this afternoon.

Mar. 18, 1917 – To-day it is a little chilly. Oscar & I went to church. Mabel & Clarence came over in the afternoon.

Mar. 20, 1917 – To-day it is just like spring. We was over to Michael Christensen's to prayer meeting in the afternoon. There wasn't very many there. The roads are a little muddy.

April 7, 1917 – To-day it is snowing and blowing. We got 8 little pigs. Martha is up at Martins. [This and next entry are probably those of Martine's.

April 6, 1917 – The canning factory burnt to-day.

Page 60

Mar. 27, 1917 – To-day the weather is very nice and the roads are pretty good. We went down to Walnut the first time in our new Ford. Anna Arentsen went with us down.

Mar. 21, 1917 – A bright baby girl is born to Mr. & Mrs. Martin Arentsen to-day.

Mar. 28, 1917 – To-day the weather is just fine. We went up to see Martin's baby. Stella [Arentsen] is working up there.

Mar. 29, 1917 – To-day I started working for Martin & Vina. I worked there 1 wk. and a half.

April 1, 1917 – To-day it is real nice weather. I was up by Martin & Vina.

April 8, 1917 – To-day it is very nice weather, but there is a little snow on the ground. I was up by Martin's all day. Eddie was also up there.

April 17, 1917 – To-day we kalsomined the ceiling in the kitchen. Arentsens took Mrs. A. B. Christensen up here. She stayed here a few days.

Page 61

April 18, 1917 – To-day we papered our kitchen. We went over to Nels Christensen's in the evening. Andrew's Anna was along.

April 20, 1917 – Ida Sahl is here making my black silk poplin skit & white crepe de chien waist.

April 22, 1917 – To-day the weather is just dandy. We went to church and went to Anton Simmonsen's after church.

April 25, 1917 – Mr. Forest Findlay & Miss Jinnie Broderson were married to-day at 5 o'clock at the Congregational parsonage. They had wedding dinner at 6 o'clock and then departed for Omaha on their honeymoon trip.

April 26, 1917 – To-day it was nice weather this forenoon. We planted potatoes below the grove. It is snowing this afternoon.

Page 62

May 6, 1917 - To-day the weather is just fine. We went to church in our car to Harlan Danish Church. In the afternoon, Ida, Minnie, Dale, Dorthy, & Elliott were up.

May 7,8, 1917 – Oscar is plowing the stalks below the windmill.

May 7, 1917 – To-day Harry Hansen left Harlan for Omaha to go to war.

May 12, 1917 – to-day the weather is fine. Oscar has just finished discing crossways below the grove.

May 20, 1917 – to-day it is real nice weather but it is blowing some. We went to church in the forenoon and all of Arentsens & Martin & Vina & Leora & Louis were here. All but Louis were here for dinner. It rained a little in the afternoon.

May 23, 1917 – To-day it is just fine weather. We papered the front room and put the carpet down. The paper has a little redish figure in it.

Page 63

Aunt Mary [Keldgord Hollenbeck] [51] died this month in New York. [written at top of page.]

Mary Keldgord Hollenbeck
(Photo by Ehrlich.)

May 28, 1917 – Oscar & I went to town to-day. I went to the dentist and had some teeth filled & pulled & 2 other teeth fixed.

May 30, 1917 – It is "Decoration Day" the 30th of May 1917. It is raining this morning. We can row our corn & our potatoes are up. The conference starts to-night & lasts till Sunday June 3rd, 1917.

May 31, 1917 Thursday – To-day it is real nice weather. We went to conference in the afternoon & evening. Fred Mund spoke in the evening.

---

[51] Mary Hollenbeck, Jacob Keldgord's sister, died May 30, 1917. She had been married to Ed Hollenbeck, who died in 1896, and lived in New York City.

June 2, 1917 Sat. – We were in all day in the afternoon. The young people all went out to Hans Jensen's & had supper.

June 3, 1917 Sunday – We went to Conference in Harlan about 10 o'clock. First it was Sunday School. Fred Mund spoke to the children. At 11 o'clock there were preaching in 4 different churches. In the afternoon it was held in the M. E. Church & evening also.

Page 64

June 12, 1917 – To-day Oscar & Mamma & I went to town in the car. I got my teeth fixed and that big piece of gold put in. I got them finished to-day.

June 15, 1917 – The weather is just fine to-day. We went out to R. J. Rassmussen's and to C. M. Petersen's.

June 16, 1917 – To-day Oscar started to cross the corn to-day. We saw a balloon come from the southwest. There were 2 men in the balloon.

July 1, 1917 – We were home all day. It is a very nice day. We went to Harlan Church in the evening to hear Children's Day program.

July 4, 1917 – To-day it is very nice weather. We went to Harlan a while by P. S. Petersen. We went out to Cuppy's Grove a while in the afternoon. There was a big crowd out in Cuppy's Grove.

Page 65

July 6, 1917 - Oscar is going to start to lay the corn by to-day. It is nice weather to-day. We are going to Walnut this afternoon. Mabel had been up a day or so. She has had the measles.

July 6, 1917 – To-day Nels H. Christensen sold his 80 acre farm to Martin Christensen for $300 an acre.

July 13, 1917 – We were out to a Red Cross ice cream social.

July 15, 1917 – To-day we went all to church. It is nice weather. Chris & Emma & children came with us home for dinner.

July 21, 1917 – Oscar & I went to Chautauqua in the evening. It sure was good. Oscar mowed hay to-day.

July 22, 1917 – The weather is hot & sultry to-day. We went all to church & went down to Mrs. Geo Arentsen's for dinner & had ice cream in the afternoon. Oscar & I went to Harlan in the evening. We heard Kryl's big band. It was just fine.

Page 66

July 23, 1917 – We are putting up hay to-day and will about finished to-morrow. Nels Christensen & Clarence are helping us. It has been hot to-day. I drove the horse for the hay fork. We made raspberry jam. My nasturnims [nasturtiums?] & pansies are blooming & the California poppy & moss roses.

July 24, 1917 – Oscar is going to haul a load of hogs for Roy. He is going to ship to Omaha. Oscar got started at 5 o'clock.

July 27, 1917 – It is very hot weather to-day. Oscar raked hay this forenoon. Martin & Lewis came up here this afternoon to help put up 2 loads of oat hay. We finished to-day making hay.

July 26, 1917 – Mrs. Back, Mary, Walter & Mabel were up here in there car for the first time. Mary had her camera along and she took some pictures.

Aug. 3, 1917 – The weather is very nice to-day. We were down to Arentsen's for Ladies Aid. There were quite a few there. We went to social in the evening down by Otto Scholbe's there was a large crowd.

Page 67

Aug. 5, 1917 – To-day the weather is nice, but a little muddy. We went to Claus Kjer's [52] funeral in the afternoon. There was a large crowd. Mabel & Walter & Melvin came along with us after the funeral and stayed a while.

Aug. 9, 1917 – The yellow crabs & black berries are ripe now.

Aug. 10, 1917 – There is going to be a Red Cross social at Roy Daw's home to-night by 2 clubs. Littleton donated a Shetland pony colt to be sold to the highest bidder. Roy Christensen bought it for $52.

Aug, 10, 1917 – Findlay's boys started to stack grain over here this afternoon. Charlie Obrect [53] died at 1 o'clock last night.

Page 68

Aug. 12, 1917 – Charlie Obrect will be buried to-morrow at 2:30 this afternoon at [the] Methodist church. He was operated upon for appendicitis the 6th of August. The appendix was bursted.

Aug. 15, 1917 – We were all to the Baptist Sunday school picnic to-day from 6 schools. There was a large crowd & a good program. Rev. Spurgeon spoke in the afternoon.

Sept. 9, 1917 – To-day the weather looks cloudy. We went out to Elkhorn to tent meetings. We went thru Kimballton for the first time.

---

[52] Claus Kjer, 1849 – 1917, was buried at Cuppy's Grove according to Find-A-Grave Memorial # 46713002.
[53] Charles A. Obrecht, Dec. 8, 1868 – Aug. 10, 1917, was buried in the Harlan Cemetery according to Find-A-Grave Memorial # 40392148.

Sept. 10, 1917 – We washed this forenoon and went to Walnut this afternoon. I got my winter hat.

Sept. 11, 1917 – We threshed this forenoon till 10 o'clock. We got 6 loads. 45 bu to acre. F.F.

April 13, 1930 – Uncle Charlie Keldgord [54] died yesterday at Los Angles Calif. He died of pneumonia. [This was written at the bottom of the page and the date specified is indeed 1930 probably by Martine.]

Page 69

Sept. 15, 1917 – To-day we were to town. It was very warm. Oscar got his new Sunday shoes with white soles. $5.00.

Sept. 16, 1917 – It is very nice weather to-day. We started about nine o'clock for Merrill's Grove church for meeting. There was a very big crowd. We were invited out to Carl Jensen's for dinner. We had a very good time.

Sept. 20, 1917 – We were in town for the soldier's reception. There was a very big crowd.

Sept. 23, 1917 – The day is just fine. We went out to Carl Sorensen's for dinner. The first time we have been there.

Sept. 24, 1917 – We washed in the forenoon and Oscar went after Uncle Nels [Nelson] in the afternoon. He stayed until Thursday. We were down in Walnut the 26th.

Sept. 22, 1917 – We went to town this evening. It was Saturday night. I got my black silk taffeta skirt. $10.50.

---

[54] Charlie also was known as Carl. California Death Index states he died on April 13, 1930, differing a day from the journal. He was buried at the West Lawn Cemetery in Omaha, Nebraska.

Page 70

Sept. 27, 1917 – We had a social in our church for the boys were now going to war from our church. They were Christian Rold, Octave Nelsen, Edwin Larsen, Virgil Lee, Russel Christensen.

Sept. 29, 1917 – To-night 575 soldiers ate supper in Harlan outside of City Hotel. We saw them march from the train and up to the square. Perry Christensen was the only Harlan boy in the bunch. They were going to Indiana.

Sept. 30, 1917 – The weather is just fine to-day. We went to church this forenoon and to Sunday School. Sahls & Stena came up here in the afternoon.

Oct. 1, 1917 – To-day is Mamma's birthday. She is 56 years old. Oscar & I are going to pick seed corn this afternoon. Nels Christensen took the 3 colts home after being over here 5 months.

Oct. 7, 1917 – To-day it is quite chilly. We were all to church and R. J. Rassmussens were here for dinner.

Page 71

Oct. 7, 1917 – It is very cold to-day. Pete Clausen & Sena Damgaard & Carsten were up here in the evening. We had a hard frost that night.

Oct. 10, 1917 - To-day the weather is just fine. We went out to Earl McDonald's in the afternoon. Their baby Alice Ann is 16 mo old.

Oct. 14, 1917 – To-day we were all to church and Sunday school. The weather is just fine. Bessie & Ed & Lester Christensen were over in the afternoon.

Oct. 20, 1917 – To-day we were in town. It was pretty cold. I got my new dark green winter coat. It cost $25.

Oct 21, 1917 – To-day the weather is a little frosty. We are going out to Fred Carlson's for dinner. We are going to have the car all closed in. A. P. Andersens & Pete, Sena & Carsten were out there. We went to Harlan church in the evening.

Page 72

We got our hydrant put in to-day, 27th, & our tank up here. [This entry was squeezed in at top.]

Oct. 28, 1917 – To-day we went to church. It is cold & cloudy & windy. We went down to Walnut after church. Mabel & Walter put their heater up to-day.

Oct. 29, 1917 – To-day it is cold & snowing a little. Oscar & I picked 95 bu to-day in 3 loads.

Oscar got his new overshoes the 3rd.

Nov. 4, 1917 – We were to church to-day. The weather is just fine. We went over to P. N Petersen's for dinner. We finished picking corn the 5th and got the cows in the stalks the same day. We picked about 850 bu of 15 acres.

Nov. 10, 1917 – To-day it is rainy & foggy. We went to town. Oscar got his new dark green suit $25.

Nov. 16, 1917 – We sold 100 bu of corn to Geo Sorensen for $1.00 a bu. The weather is just fine.

Nov. 25, 1917 - To-day it is windy & cold. We sold 15 spring pigs to Geo Sorensen for 18₵ lb. average 120 lb.

Page 73

Nov. 15, 1917 – To-day it is cloudy. We are going down to Walnut & maybe I am going to stay.

Nov. 27, 1917 – Her name is Lela Margaret. This morning a baby girl was born to Mr. & Mrs. W. F. Larsen. Martha is working down there.

Dec. 2, 1917 – Tonight Ma & I are alone home. Michael Christensens were over here. [This must be Oscar writing the next few entries.]

Dec. 15, 1917 – To-day Ed & Lester [Christensen] were over here this afternoon. Ed bought my duck coat.

Dec. 7, 1917 – I went to town to get our groceries from Ohio. It snowed all the time I was there.

Dec. 18, 1917 – To-day Mamma & Oscar went down to Walnut to bring me home. I had been down there 3 wks & 2 days. The roads were pretty good.

Dec. 19, 1917 – To-day a baby boy was born to Mr. & Mrs. Geo [Stella Arentsen] Mickel of Walnut.

Dec. 20 – To-day Christian Rold, Russel, C. Anton Swenson [Ed Larsen, Octave Nelson added above.] went to war.

Page 74

Dec. 25, 1917 – To-day we are all alone home all day. It is real nice weather. We went to Harlan Danish church to hear the Xmas program. It was real good. The church was just full.

Dec. 29, 1917 – To-day it is very cold & frosty. It froze 28 below last night. Oscar drove Nels Christensen's car to town to-day. Clarence is going to stay in town.

Dec. 31, 1917 – To-day it is nice weather. Nels Christensen's
came over here this afternoon. He butchered a pig for us.

1918

Jan. 1, 1918 – To-day it is real nice weather. Everything was white. We went down to Walnut. I saw Mickel's baby the first time.

Jan. 4, 1918 – To-day the weather is nice, not a bit cold. We got our new alarm clock. We were out to Bergs a little while.

Jan. 6, 1918 – To-day it is snowing & blowing. It is 27 years since mother came to this country.

Page 75

Jan. 14, 1918 – A baby boy was born to Ellis Gearharts to-day. It weighed 10 lbs. .

Jan. 13, 1918 – We were over by Mike Christensen's for dinner to-day. It was nice weather. We drove in the car.

Jan. 16, 1918 – Mary E. Christensen & Jack French were married at noon.

Jan. 20, 1918 – The weather is rather cold to-day. P. N. Petersens were here for dinner to-day. They went down to Geo Sorensen's in the evening.

Jan. 26, 1918 – To-day it is zero, it is snowing fast and drifting also.

Jan. 23, 1918 - We were down in Walnut to-day. It was Mabel's 24th birthday. Lela was 8 weeks old. It was melting some and the roads were quite muddy.

Jan. 25, 1918 – We first started to use of the corn crib.

Jan. 26, 1918 – We got 9 eggs to-day.

Feb. 8, 1918 – Charlie Lansman & wife are proud parents of a baby girl born to-day. [A note above this entry states "She died when she was 2 yrs old."]

Feb. 10, 1918 – To-day is nice weather but it is melting some. Martin & Vina & baby were up here for dinner. We went down to Geo Sorensen to-night. Nels Christensen's were also there.

Page 76

Feb. 14, 1918 - To-day it is sleeting & snowing. Oscar took me up to Martin [Arentsen]'s. I helped her sew some house dresses & for Elaine. I came home Saturday afternoon the 16th. Oscar hauled hogs for Forest to-day.

Feb. 18, 1918 – To-day it is thawing. We got Dolly to-day. It is Nels Christensen's sale to-morrow.

Feb. 19, 1918 – To-day it is very cold. It is drifting & snowing. It is Nels C. sale to-day. Everything sold pretty good. Hens bro't $1.30 to $1.40 a piece. Roosters $3 a piece. We bot the mower. $11.00.

Feb. 21, 1918 – Mamma & Oscar were to town in the top buggy. They drove Dolly & Babe together for the first time to town. The roads are pretty rough.

Feb. 21, 1918 – We were over to Nels C. to-night, the last time over on their farm.

Feb. 22, 1918 – We were over to P.N. Petersen this afternoon. The roads were muddy, the last time on that place.

Page 77

Mar. 1, 1918 – Martin Christensen's moved over on Nels C. place.

Feb. 22, 1918 – We were over to P. Jespersen's last night. It was moonlight. I got a crochet pattern the hardanger lace.

March 1, 1918 – I was up by Martins to-day. They moved west of town on Vina's mother's place. I stayed out there till March 5, 1918.

March 6, 1918 – We were up to visit Forest & Jennie [Findlay] last night.

March 17, 1918 – To-day the weather is just fine. We were to church to-day. [Rev. Ewald Nielsen] preached. We were down to Arentsen's for dinner and some of us went up to Hoiriis' [55] in the afternoon to see Dean. He had broke his leg 2 or 3 days before. We were also to church in the evening.

March 20, 1918 – To-day Oscar started to disc the 15 acres. It is very warm weather.

March 21, 1918 – To-day it is very windy. We went to town in the car with side curtains off. I got my black summer hat trimmed with blue ribbon. Oscar got his hat also.

Page 78

Mar. 24, 1918 – To-day we were to church in the forenoon. We went down to Walnut in the afternoon.

Mar. 25, 1918 – We got our garden planted to-day & got a new fence around it. I planted radishes & lettuce & onion sets.

---

[55] Rev. Alexander V. Hoiriis ministered at Cuppy's Gove from 1913 to 1919.

Mar. 30, 1918 – To-day Oscar & Mamma were in town this forenoon to get new transmission bands put in the car. In the evening we went to Walnut to get Mabel & Walter & children.

Mar. 31, 1918 Easter Sunday – To-day it is windy. We went all to church in the forenoon but Mamma. We took them back home in the afternoon. We were over to Mike Christensen's in the evening.

April 4, 1918 – To-day is nice weather. It is a little chilly. We went to Ladies Aid at John Vinding's. There were quite a few there. We burned stalks below the windmill to-night.

April 7, 1918 – We went to church to-day. Ed White & Senator Kimball of Council Bluffs spoke. Anna Arentsen went with us home for dinner. We also went to church in the evening. They had a missionary program.

Page 79

The water came up in our cistern to-day. We cleaned it to-day.

April 15, 1918 – To-day it is raining a little. Oscar plowed this afternoon below the grove. I planted peas to-day.

April 16, 1918 – Last night we had the first good spring rain. To-day is nice weather. We cleaned the pantry. I kalsomined it over twice with yellow.

April 18, 1918 – Oscar got thru plowing to-day. I finished papering & cleaning my room to-day.

May 2, 1918 – To-day we were out to Karl Kjer's to Ladies aid. There were quite a few there.

May 4, 1918 – We were to town in the evening to telephone meeting.

1918

May 5, 1918 – To-day we went out to see Martin & Vina [Arentsen]. Elaine can walk now. Luella Nelson & Carmel Erickson were there.

Page 80

May 7, 1918 –This afternoon Oscar started to plant corn. The first time he run a planter. May 10th he finished planting 26 acres.

May 5, 1918 – To-day Pete Clausen & Sena Damgaard went to Des Moines and were married at the Lutheran College.

May 12, 1918 – Yesterday Arentsens & John Nelsons got a telegram that Mrs. Andrew Christensen died. She was operated on about a wk before. Mrs. Geo Arentsen & Anna, Old Mrs. Nelson & Mrs. John Nelson went on the 2 o'clock to be present at the funeral. [56]

May 28 – Louis Berg went to Camp Dodge. [Rev.] Ewald Nelson died June 5, 1918.

June 3, 1918 – To-day it is real nice weather. We washed. Oscar finished plowing the 8 acres the first time. We planted pumpkins & water melons yesterday.

June 12, 1918 – To-day the weather is nice. Oscar is plowing across the 8 acres. We are going to have Bible Study here to-night. We are going down to get Mabel & children to-morrow and also Ladies Aid at Frank Hansen.

Page 81

---

[56] Mrs. Arentsen was sister to Andrew Christensen. Andrew may have been in Modesto, CA by this time. His wife was a Nelson.

June 15, 1918 – We were all in town to-day. It is very hot. Mabel & children were along. We had the baby's picture taken. She is almost 7 mo.

June 17, 1918 – To-day Andrew Nelson built that stall in the horse barn. We took Mabel, Melvin & Lela home to-night.

June 28, 1918 – Paul Kemp & Cecelia Ohms were married.

July 3, 1918 – To-day is very warm & windy & dusty. We had our first spring chicken for dinner.

July 4, 1918 – Frank Haleson & Louis Berg was home to-day. To-day it is cloudy. We went out to the grove to picnic. It started to rain after the program, so we went home. Rev. Roberts spoke.

July 7, 1918 – To-day it has been cloudy & chilly all day. We didn't have any meeting at our church. They went out to Merrill's Grove church for 25 yrs jubilee & [Rev. Niel S. Lawdahl's] silver wedding. Louis Berg was also home to-day. He went with Arentsens out there, We were over to Mike Christensen's in the afternoon.

Page 82

July 8, 1918 - To-day it is warm weather. We started to put up the oats hay down by the wind mill. Mrs. Martin Christensen was over here a little while this afternoon. Our late cherries & raspberries are all gone. We canned 22 qts of raspberries this year.

July 13, 1918 - This forenoon occurred the marriage of Nels Block & Jennie Erickson. They left immediately for Des Moines.

July 19, 1918 – This afternoon occurred the wedding of Helen Christensen to Jens Jensen at 2 o'clock. They left 4 o'clock for Des Moines.

July 16, 1918 – We were to a social at C. J. Rold's to-night. We went with Ivan & Grace. The party was in honor of Arthur S. Knudson, Leslie L. Edwards, Thorvald Andersen, Arthur Andersen. Ed Larsen was there from Fort Worden. [57] Prof [Niel] S. Lawdahl, wife & Naomi were there. We had ice cream & cake.

July 31, 1918 – Ida Sahl came up here this afternoon to make Mama's black & white lawn dress and Mabel's gingham dress with plain blue collar & cuffs. We took her home Friday.

Page 83

Aug. 4, 1918 – To-day we went to church in the forenoon & evening. Rev. Ralph Jensen spoke in the evening. It was very hot to-day. The thermometer was up to 108 to-day.

July 26, 1918 – To-day it has been warm weather. There went 200 boys to Camp Pike at 6 o'clock on the Rock Island. There were many people in town. They ate supper south of the post office. They had a program & several bands played. Some of the boys were: Harry Sahl, Svante, Hans Petersen, Ora Argotsinger, Arthur Knudson , Leslie Edwards, Thorwald Anderson, Jack French, Paul Kemp, Harry Petersen, Nels Block.

Aug. 8, 1918 – To-day Ivan Christensen shot old Gloss & Oscar buried her. We got $4.50 for hide.

Aug. 9, 1918 – E. S. Anthony [59] died the 7th and was buried this afternoon from the A[merican] Baptist church.

---

[57] This may refer to the Fort Worden in Washington.

[59] Ephriam S. Anthony, Jul. 1852 - 1918, was buried in the Harlan Cemetery according to Find-A-Grave Memorial # 8415034.

Aug. 9, 1918 – Old Andrew Fredricksen died to-day, about 9 o'clock in the evening & was buried the 13th Danish Baptist Church [Rev.] M[artin] A. Wesgard.

Page 84

Aug. 14, 1918 – Geo Gilletts threshed this afternoon till about 4 o'clock. Oscar helped up there and down by Roy's till evening. They threshed all day down there till 5 o'clock. They had 60 acres of grain.

Aug. 14, 1918 – To-day John Fredrickson got a telegram that their boy Louis [60] had died from wounds July 20th in France.

Aug. 10, 1918 – Oscar & I drove down to Walnut to get Mabel & Family. They stayed over Sunday. We took them back on Sunday evening.

Aug. 21, 1918 – To-day it is windy & dusty. We went to fair to-day. There was a very large crowd down there. We sure was tired & dirty when we got home. Oscar went in the next day to see the auto races.

Aug. 24, 1918 – We went to town this afternoon. It is very hot weather. Mamma got some blue percale goods for an every day dress at 25¢ a yd. an for an apron for me of the same kind.

Page 85

Aug 25, 1918 – To-day it is very nice weather. We went up to P. N. Petersen's near Irwin. Mike's kids & Ed Andersen & family were also there. In the afternoon we drove thru Irwin & out to the Oak Hill cemetery to see Aunt Sena [Nelson Larsen]'s [61]

---

[60] Louie C. Fredericksen, 1899 – 1918, was buried at the Harlan Cemetery according to Find-A-Grave Memorial # 38683172.
[61] Aunt Sena was Martine's sister, Sena Nelsen, married to Lars Larsen. Pete Nelsen may have been a brother, Christen Peter Nelsen.

grave & Pete Nelsen's grave. Mamma hadn't seen that cemetery in 22 yrs [62]. The roads were very good.

Aug. 26, 1918 [in margin] – Elsie Erickson & Martin Mortensen were married at Des Moines to-day.

Aug. 28, 1918 – To-day Mrs. Geo Arentsen, Elmer, Anna, Stella & Jim Berg from Calif. Came up to visit us this afternoon. We went down to Geo Rassmusen's to get Mabel Berg. She stayed till Saturday forenoon Aug. 31.

Lars and Sena Larsen
(Photo by Dammand.)

Aug. 30, 1918 – To-day is the Red Cross Sale from Monroe Township. We went out in the afternoon a while. There was a big crowd out ther. They sold horses, cattle, sheep, hogs, chickens & other things. They made about $2200. They also sold ice cream & cake.

Page 86

Aug. 31, 1918 – Oscar & I & Ivan & Grace went with us down to C. Knudsen to a party on the boys that are going the 5th of Sept. They are Roy Larsen, Roy [illegible] Oleson, Howard Thompsen, Herman Nelsen & Hallie Bartrug from Harlan, Harold Findlay, Roy Reinhart, Otto Carlson, Henry Ohms, Pete Claus.

---

[62] Based on this, Martine would have been to the Oak Hill cemetery in 1896. Sena may have died by that time.

Sept. 5, 1918 – To-day they had doings for the boys that leave for Camp Dodge in the morning. The Earling band played and Mr. Orchard spoke in the afternoon. There is going about 70 or 73.

Sept. 6, 1918 – This morning we went to town half past 5 o'clock to see the boys leave. There was a big crowd down by the train. Howard Thompsen came home the 14th. He had a weak heart.

Sept. 12, 1918 – Oscar registered to-day by Center school [63]. Ida Sahl came up here to-day to sew my blue silk taffeta dress with chiffon sleeves.

Sept. 14, 1918 – This afternoon Mamma & Oscar went to town. Mrs. C. E. Marvin came with the home to stay over Sunday. We went to Walnut this evening. Anna & Claude live near Trumbull Nebr.

Page 87

Sept. 17, 1918 – To-day it is blowing hard. Oscar & I picked 4 sacks of white seed corn.

Sept. 16, 1918 – To-day a baby girl 8 lb. was born to Mrs. Mike Rath. Mr. Rath is fighting in France, but just now he is in the hospital.

Sept. 22, 1918 – To-day it is very nice weather. We went out to Elk Horn to Harvest Feast. Cuppy's Grove, Harlan, Merrill's Grove were out there. It was held in the new Baptist church which they bot recently.

---

[63] It isn't clear if this was school registration, or draft registration. No draft registration for Oscar Keldgord has been found.

Sept. 29, 1918 – It is nice weather to-day. Mabel & Family & Walter's folks came up here to visit. They came in Jim's car.

Oct. 1, 1918 – It is raining a little to-day. Mamma & Oscar went to town to get his questionnaire filled out. Ivan went in to-day too.

Oct. 3, 1918 – To-day we went to town. I had a tooth filled. We started to pick the 8 acres.

Page 86 #2 [page numbers 86 and 87 are reused.]

Oct. 1, 1918 – Russel McDonald [64] died to-day of pneumonia at his home west of Harlan.

Oct. 3, 1918 – Everett Gillette [65] died of pneumonia & influenza Oct. 3rd at Massachusetts. He was buried Oct. 7, 1918, the service was held at the house. Rev. Trennery spoke.

Oct. 9, 1918 – Roy's man started to pick yesterday afternoon. We are going to finish picking the 8 acres below the grove this afternoon about 3 o'clock.

Oct. 10, 1918 – To-day it is nice weather. We are busy picking corn. We are picking in the west part of the 12 acres.

Nov. 12, 1918 – To-day Chris Thorgesen was killed by a train at nine o'clock. He was in his Ford.

Page 87 #2

[64] Russell McDonald, June 22, 1889 – Oct. 1, 1918, was buried at the Shelby Cemetery according to Find-A-Grave Memorial # 48052682.
[65] Everette Eliga Gillett, May 19, 1896 – Oct. 3, 1918, was buried in the Harlan Cemetery according to Find-A-Grave Memorial # 38683251.

Oct. 25, 1918 – To-day we finished picking corn. It started to sleet before we got to the end. We sold 91 bu right from the field to Geo Sorensen for $1.25 per bu.

Oct. 31, 1918 – To-day it is cloudy & cold. We went down to Walnut to visit. We hadn't been down there for 6 wks. Lela can stand alone now, but she can't walk yet.

Nov. 3, 1918 – To-day it is nice weather. We were up to Back's for dinner. Thule Jensens, Nels Jensens & Svensens were there. Helen was home.

Nov. 4, 1918 – We were in to say good bye to Elmer Arentsen to-day. He left for Ames. Fred Mortensen was buried to-day.

Nov. 8, 1918 – To-day we bo't a sorrel colt of Geo Sorensen for $120 named Goldie. Oscar went to town in the lumber wagon after coal with Dolly & Babe.

Nov. 10, 1918 – To-day Mr. and Mrs. C. Sahl was up here in the afternoon. It is nice weather.

Nov. 11, 1918 – [Above this entry was written: There was a big crowd in town. They had a program & the band played.] To-day they got a telegram from Wash D.C. that war was over. The whistle started to blow & bells started to ring about 3 or 4 o'clock. Oscar took 7 spring pigs in to-day.$16.50.

Page 88

Nov. 14, 1918 - To-day Aunt Minnie [Nelson Christensen] [66] died of pneumonia in Calif. All of the rest of them are sick of the "flu" now. [67]

---

[66] Aunt Minnie married Lars Peter Christensen and lived in Selma, California.

Nov. 22, 1918 – To-day it is snowing some, the first time this fall. Oscar went to town in the car to get it fixed. The valves ground, new transmission band put in. We were over to Martin's G. last night. We played on the piano & sang.

Nov. 27, 1918 – Lela [Larsen] is 1 yr old to-day. To-day is real nice weather. We are sawing wood to-day. Mike & Ed & Martin C. is helping. It is Geo Sorensen's saw and engine.

Nov. 28, 1918 – To-day is Thanksgiving. We were alone home all day. It is about 5 in of snow on the ground.

Nov. 29, 1918 – To-day Mrs. Hans Rassmusen died east of here of pneumonia. She left 4 children.

Nov. 29, 1918 – Mrs. Forest Findlay has been sick nearly 2 wks. She is better to-day. Miss Kern is the nurse.

Nov. 30, 1918 – Etta Fredricksen [68]is very sick to-day. Mama & Oscar were to town to-day in the car. Etta died Dec. 2 or 3rd.

A baby boy was born to Mr. and Mrs. James Kemp last night. To-day is the 1st day of Dec. 1918.

Kemps, Bamseys & Ivan has the "flu". Etta F was buried to-day. Dec. 5, 1918.

All of Martin C's has the flu but Mrs., Dale & Hughie. All of Bamseys have it too.

To-day is the 8th of Dec. 1918. We are home, but Oscar went down to Carmichael's this afternoon. Mrs. Jens Jacobson [69] died

---

[67] A daughter of Minnie's, Ida Christensen, age 14, died a few days after her mother.

[68] Etta Mae Frederickson, Mar 13, 1891 – Dec. 3, 1918, was buried in Harlan Cemetery according to Find-A-Grave Memorial # 38683177.

this forenoon of flu following pneumonia. All the rest are sick but Mr. Jacobsen.

[Three sheets are cut out at this point. The first half of the next sheet contains what appear to be some arithmetic problems. The next entry is dated Dec. 11, 1918, so few if any days were lost.]

Page 95

Elmer Arentsen came home from Ames to-night. Dec. 11, 1918.

To-day is the 12th of Dec 1918. Melvin is 4 yrs old. It is raining little. We hauled straw & split wood. To-day.

Dec. 13, 1918 – to-day Carrie Petersen [70] died to-day. She was 16 yrs old. She died down by Geo Sorensen's. Harry Hansen also died to-day of the "flu". They are going to be buried Sunday the 15th.

Mrs. Clarence Tobias [71] died the 15th of Dec. 1918. Hazel Gillette [72] died the 13th.

Dec. 18, 1918 - Oscar & I went over to Sam Mickelson and got the first vaccination [73] and all of Sam's & Nels Jensens. Dr. Bisgard did it.

---

[69] Dorothea Jacobsen, 1879 – 1918, was buried in the Harlan Cemetery according to Find-A-Grave Memorial # 38788991.

[70] Carrie Petersen, 1902 – 1918, was buried at Cuppy's Grove according to Find-A-Grave Memorial # 98480117.

[71] Daisy Tobias, Mar. 22, 1891 – Dec. 15, 1918, was buried at Cuppy's Grove according to Find-A-Grave Memorial # 98485589.

[72] Hazel V. Gillett, 1894 – 1918, was buried in the Harlan Cemetery according to Find-A-Grave Memorial # 38683253.

[73] The cause of the 1918 influenza epidemic wasn't known at the time. A vaccine was developed, but its effectiveness has been doubted. There are no entries stating that Oscar or Martha got the flu.

Dec. 23, 1918 – To-day it is snowing and is very cold. We washed. This afternoon we got our second shot over by [Sam's?].

Dec. 25 – To-day it is clear, but cold. We were alone home all day. Ivan & Oscar are hunting rabbits.

Page 96 Memorandum

Dec. 26, 1918 – To-day it is real nice. We went down to Arentsen's in the car. The roads were rough.

Dec. 28, 1918 – To-day Elmer & Eddie butchered a hog for us. They came with their tank heater.

Dec. 31, 1918 – To-day it is very cold & blowing. Oscar & I went to town in the car to-day. We were in by Nels Christensen's for dinner. They played on the player piano. Kimball. We were also over by Stena.

1919

Jan. 1, 1919 – It is very cold to-day. 10 below. We went down skating in John Nelson's pond. Lillian C. went with us. There is some snow on the ground. Kemps upset in the sled & the horses run away.

Jan. 2, 1919 – Oscar hauled 8 hogs down to Geo Sorensen's. $13 a piece.

Jan. 12, 1919 – To-day it is nice weather overhead but it is muddy. It is melting the snow. We were to town yesterday in the car.

Jan. 14, 1919 – To-day it is nice weather. Oscar went with Geo to H. P. Hansen's sale.

Jan. 15, 1919 – It is also nice to-day. It is almost like spring. The snow is nearly all gone. I sewed Ma's 2 gingham checked aprons yesterday. We got the goods at [Bemke's?] sale.

Page 97

Jan. 19, 1919 – To-day it is nice weather but the roads are bad some places. We were down in Walnut to-day.

Jan. 23, 1919 – To-day is cloudy & some muddy. Mama & Oscar went to town in the car. They bo't our first big rug and library table. Harold Findlay came home to-day about half past eight in the evening. He is discharged.

Jan. 27, 1919 – To-day it is nice weather. We went to town & bo't a rug for the big room or front room. We got it at Boysen & Schaack $45. The first rug we have ever bo't

Jan. 28, 1919 – To-day it is just fine weather. Mr. & Mrs. Berg & Mr. & Mrs. Mike G. Rath were here for dinner. The baby was 4 mo old. We went out to Berg's in the evening. They had a surprise on Mike.

Jan. 30, 1919 – Yesterday we shelled 115 bu of corn. Sold to D. J. Carmichael at $2.55 per bu. Sam Mickelsen shelled it. Ivan & Oscar hauled it in 2 loads. Us kids went to the show that night.

Jan. 31, 1919 – To-day it is a little chilly. Oscar hauled our 3 ront pigs over to Martin C. at $13 a piece.

Page 98 – 102 Memory Gems [These are a collection of quotes and poems, not included here.]

Page 103 – 111 Recipes [These are not included here.]

Page 112 Memorandum

Feb. 1, 1919 – To-day it is Saturday. We were in town in the afternoon. Mabel & Walter & Melvin & Lela came up in Jim's car. They stayed over night. They went home Sunday afternoon. It rained some & the roads were slippery. I got my dark brown stocking to-day.

Feb. 6, 1919 – We got 16 eggs to-day. It is snowing and drifting.

Feb. 14, 1919 – Our cows were in the barn nearly all day. [At top]. To-day it is almost a blizzard. It rained all night the other night. Now it is snow on every thing. It is freezing to-night. Ivan & Grace were over there this afternoon. The mailman didn't come to-day. It has drifted so bad.

Feb. 16, 1919 – It is Sunday to-day. Ma and I were alone home all day. Oscar went horse back riding. The roads are to bad for cars. In the evening, Geo Sorensen's came up her. Mrs. Wilson was along.

Feb. 17, 1919 – To-day it is fine weather. Ivan shot old King. We sold the hide, got $4.50 for it of Reyart.

Feb. 23, 1919 – It is nice weather over head to-day. The roads are muddy. Oscar & I went to church with the team & buggy the first time since Sept. There wasn't very many people there.

Page 113 Day Book

Feb. 22, 1919 – Paul Kemp came home from Camp Dodge to-night on the 10 o'clock. Richard went after him on horse back. He has been over in France.

Feb. 24, 1919 – To-day Oscar & Ivan and Geo's hired man drove Geo's hogs over on the Wilson place. They drove 150 of them. It was rainy in the forenoon & it turned cold in the afternoon.

To-day Geos moved all the house hold goods, Tuesday the 25th. It froze hard last night. Oscar took the women folks over. Elmer Steel's moved down on Chris Hansen's old place to-day.

Feb. 26, 1919 – To-day it is very cold and it is snowing some. Oscar is 19 yrs old to-day. We washed also, but it was too windy & cold to hang them out. We got 22 eggs to-day.

Mar. 1, 1919 – To-day it is chilly. The wind is in the south. The roads are awfully rough. Oscar went to town in the top buggy & Babe & Doll.

Mar. 5, 1919 – To-day it is nice weather, but a little cold. Oscar & I hauled straw in the barn, and this afternoon we went to town to get my first wisdom tooth pulled & another filled. Oscar bo't a new front tire of [Borth's?], the first new one for our ford.

Page 114

Mar. 6, 1919 – A. P. Andersen [74] died this morning at his home on Sixth St. of Heart failure

Mar. 12 – We were in town in the car to-day. The roads were pretty good. Emil Fredricksen [75] died to-day of "flu" following pneumonia at his home 4 miles north of Harlan. Rubina has the flu now. He will be buried to-morrow. Elmer Kelgord [76] came to Harlan to-day from Calif. Stella [Keldgord Plummer] & her children are down by Plummer's.

Chris Keldgord Family - 1890 - L to R: Elmer, Christian, Annie, Martine, Christine, and Stella. Clarence not born yet. (Photo by Dammand.)

---

[74] A. Anderson, 1866 – 1919, was buried at the Harlan Cemetery according to Find-A-Grave Memorial # 38536049.
[75] Emil Frederickson, 1882 – 1919, was buried in the Harlan Cemetery according to Find-A-Grave Memorial # 38683176.
[76] Elmer and Stella Keldgord were cousins to Martha, children of Chris Keldgord.

Mar. 13 – To-day Martin & Ivan brought our 3 yr old colt over here. We bought it of him $140. Her name is Beauty.

Mar. 15 – To-day it is raining. We heard a robin & meadow lark and black birds. It has thundered also. It's just like spring.

Mar. 21 – To-day Oscar went in after Stella Plummer [77] & Raymond & Billie. They visited out here till Sunday the 23rd. Clyde Obrect came after them.

Mar. 24 – To-day is Monday, we washed, and got it all dry. The 25th we have 3 hens setting. We haven't planted any garden yet. The grass is getting green.

Page 115 - 1919

Mar. 27 – To-day it has been chilly. The roads were pretty good. We went down to Walnut. We had the top down on the Ford.

Mar. 28 – We were in town to-night to Hulsebus' auto show. They had free show at the Lyric and jazz band at Hulsebus'. It sure was swell music.

Mar. 29 – To-day it is warm. I planted sweet peas, radishes & lettuce.

Mar. 31 – To-day Martin & Ivan helped Oscar hitch the colts on the disc. He worked them all afternoon. They worked fine. It was for oats on the 12 acres.

April 4, 1919 - To-day is my 24th birthday. It is nice weather. Oscar is discing. I have a bad cold. Mrs. Martha Christensen, Grace & Hughie were over a little while in the afternoon. I got a white crepe de cien handkerchief.

---

[77] Stella Mae Keldgord married Joseph Carl Plummer on Feb. 2, 1907. Stella died in Nebraska in 1923. Stella was daughter of Chris Keldgord.

Apr. 9 – To-day it is raining. It also rained last night. We had 5 little pigs last night. The grass is getting so green.

Apr. 8 – A baby boy was born to Mr. & Mrs. Earl Caddock to-day. Mr. Caddock is still in France. His name is Earl Jr.

Page 116 – 1919 Daybook

Apr. 14 – Mrs. James M. Jensen died at Rochester Minn this morning following an operation. The funeral was held at the Danish Baptist Church in Harlan the 17th.

Apr. 20 – To-day is Easter Sunday. It is nice weather. We went to church and to Walnut in the afternoon.

Apr. 21 – It rained some to-day. We put the separator out in the cob house to-day. We have 19 little pigs and 36 little chickens.

Apr. 23 – We have 47 little chicks. Ivan, Bernice, Grace, Oscar & I went over to Andrew Christensen's last night to hear their player, Hallet & Davis. It started to thunder & lightening when we had been there half an hour. We got as far as the river bridge [78] when it started to pour down. We sat in the car during all the storm. We got home about 1 o'clock.

May 3 – It is nice & warm to-day. We went to town this afternoon. I got my new spring coat. It is gray & white fine stripes $20.

Page 117 – 1919

May 8 – To-day is nice warm weather. The first warm weather for about 2 wks. Oscar is plowing the eight acres below the grove. We are cleaned Ma's & my bedroom to-day. The plum &

---

[78] The creek was to the west, but the Nishnabotna River was just a mile east.

apple & cherry trees are in bloom. The peas & parsley, carrots, beets are up and the sweet peas too.

May 8 – It was very nice weather last night. We went to Chase-Lister. The play was "Tempest and Sunshine." It sure was a good show. Oscar will finish plowing to-day the 9th. Harold Findlay started to plant corn yesterday.

May 12 – To-day is nice weather. Oscar is discing the 20 acres. He disced nearly all of it to-day. This afternoon Karsten Clausen was up to see us. He was discharged and came home the 9th from Camp Dodge. He had been down in Alabama.

May 17 – To-day Old Trena Fredricksen [79] died at Alex Smith's. She was 91 yrs old in March.

Page 118 – 1919

May 18 – To-day is nice weather. Mabel & Walter & children came home in Jim's car. After dinner we all went to town to visit Elmer & Sue [Keldgord] & children. It rained in the evening.

May 19 – It has been nice weather to-day. Oscar planted corn by the windmill. He will finish planting to-morrow. I put tomatoe plants out to-day. The peas are big & we have used come of our radishes & onions.

May 28 – This evening Sylvia Rold & Alvin Christensen, Marian Rold & Arnold Jacobson were united in marriage at the brides parents. Mr. & Mrs. Christian Rold.

May 29 – The "Home coming" doings was held to-day in Harlan for the home coming solders. They all marched down Baldwin

[79] Alex Smith was married to Hannah Frederickson, daughter of Catrine and Andrew according to the 1925 Iowa census for Hannah Smith in Harlan, Iowa. They were Baptists. No burial location has been identified.

Street & floats & decorated cars came down Baldwin from each Township in Shelby County. It sure was a swell parade. They marched down to the Fair grounds. The soldiers had supper in a big tent at 6:30.

Page 119 – 1919

They had a dance in the evening. There was a very large crowd. It was so warm & dusty.

June 2 – To-day it is a little rainy. We paper the kitchen. It is kinda brick figure in it. We kalsomined the ceiling. We are going to wash the woodwork to-morrow.

June 15 – To-day it is nice weather altho' it looks a little rainy. We went to church. It was "Children's Day". They had a program. I was in a big dialogue. They had a very nice program. Oscar & I went to church to-night. I wore my new black oxfords for the first time to-day.

June 5 – To-day Russel E. Christensen & Hazel M. Christensen were united in marriage. The groom has a place ready for them to move in. Rev. [Alexander] Hoiriis married them.

June 17 – It has been very warm to-day. Oscar plowed corn with Doll & Beaut. The first time he plowed corn with the colts. He will finished plowed the first time day after tomorrow.

Page 120 – 1919

June 19 – To-night the young people of Cuppy's Grove came and surprised Mr. & Mrs. Alvin Christensen. It was a little rainy. We played out doors & had a good time. We had ice cream, lemonade and cake.

1919

June 24, 1919 – To-night it is very nice weather. The young people went down to surprise Mr. and Mrs. Russel Christensen. We played out doors & had ice cream, lemondade, & cake.

June 29 – To-day is Sunday. It is real nice weather. Last night we went down after Mabel & family. We all went to church to-day but Mama. Edward & Leonard Petersen were here also over night. They went home Sunday night.

July 1 – To-day Oscar mowed some hay. I picked raspberries. Oscar is going to start to lay by the corn to-day.

July 9 – It is very hot to-day. Oscar will finish laying by the 20 acres. We have only canned 6 quts of raspberries this year. We took of the beans the first time yesterday. We have put up 4 acres of hay.

Page 121 – 1919

We canned 3 quts of beets to-day.

July 10 – It is very nice weather. It has been hot to-day. Oscar finished laying by the corn to-day 35 acres. Oscar & I went to town to-night to hear the band. Vernon Plummer is staying out here now.

July 13 – It rained hard last night. The river down east was way over its banks, nearly up to Mike's barn. We didn't go to church. We went up to Sahl's a while in the afternoon.

July 16 – To-day we put up the 2 acres. We got 5 loads off of that. We are thru making hay now. We got in 23 loads in all.

July 4 – To-day we were out in the grove. There were quite a few there. The B.Y.P.U. had a stand. They made $42.00. I helped in the stand 2 hrs. We was out in the evening a while too.

July 5 – Backs were down by Helen & Jens to-day. When coming back from there, they upset & mashed the car up quite a bit. Mrs. got both her hands hurt. Mr. got his leg hurt. Mabel got her leg cut above the ankle. They had a speshalist operate on her. She is down in Atlantic hospital. They had another girl with them from Omaha. She just got a few [scratches].

Page 122 – 1919

July 18 – To-day is just fine weather. Jens Sorensen is cutting our grain. The oats are pretty good.

July 22 – Oscar hauled in the last 2 sows to-day. They 205 lbs a piece at 20¢ a lb. We got $82 for them.

We sold 3 before they averaged about 225 lbs a piece at 19¢ a lb.

July 25 – It is blowing and is very hot to-day. Mama & Oscar went to town this forenoon & bo't a new lumber wagon of C. J. Hansen for $100.

July 27 – It is very warm weather to-day & dusty. We went up to Pete Petersen's by Irwin. Tuckers were there from Kirkman. John Spensers were also there. It started to look like rain about 6 o'clock so we had to hurry home, but we didn't get any rain.

Aug. 1 – The bridge gang is down her by the bridge. They have started to dig trenches. They have 3 tents in our pasture. There are 4 men with the gang.

Aug. 8 – We went to town to-day. I got the silk meseline goods for my skirt. Mrs. Wilson is sewing it. It has a blue & brown stripe.

Page 123 – 1919

Aug. 10 – It is real nice weather to-day. We went to church & we went down to Knudson's for dinner & then went down to Walnut after dinner.

Aug. 11 – We canned a box of peaches to-day. 11 quts. The 19th we canned another box of peaches. 11 ½ quts.

Aug. 15 – It is nice weather, altho a little threatning, but it didn't rain after all. We threshed out of shock this year. The first time we had all the oats for nearly 15 yrs. We had 12 acres of oats and got 490 bu. We had 15 men for dinner. Stena Sahl was out a few days. The red steer calf was born 17th or 18th of July.

Aug. 21 – To-day is the last day of fair. It has been real nice weather. There sure was a big crowd. They had auto races. But they wasn't very good.

Aug. 27 – (Wed.) The conference starts to-night at Cuppy's grove. We wasn't there till Thursday afternoon. Oscar took Ma out there. We was there Friday night. Rev [Henry A. Reichenbach] & Prof S[oren] P. Fogdall spoke.

Aug. 28 – Thurs. This afternoon was the Ladies meeting. Mamma was out there at the conference.

Page 124 – 1919

Aug. 30 – This afternoon was the young people's session. Elsie Sorensen from Co Bluffs gave a talk. Morris Nelson from Sac City gave also a good talk on Christianity. I went with Sahls out there. Oscar was over to Mike's threshing.

Aug. 31 – It is Sunday to-day. We was out to the church all day. Rev. [Julius] A. Jensen from Harlan spoke in the forenoon. Mrs. Turner was the cook out there. There was 6 girls to wait on tables. I was one of them. We served 150 people for dinner. Some of the people went home for dinner & some had their lunch along. There sure was a large crowd all day. They sold ice cream. S. C. Larsen from Michigan, Henningsen from Alta spoke in the afternoon. [Rev.] Jacob Vinding spoke out in the grove to a big crowd. Rev. A[ndrew] Petersen from Elk Horn spoke in the evening.

Sept. 3 – To-day the bridge gang are down finishing running the concrete. They were four men here for dinner & supper. They finished the bridge to-day. It took them nearly 5 wks.

Page 125 – 1919

Sept. 4 – It is cloudy to-day. Oscar started about half past seven to take the cement mixer out about 6 miles northeast of here. He hauled it out with Doll & Babe.

Sept. 14 – To-day Oscar went in after Elmer & Sue [Keldgord] & children & Elmer's mother. They were here for dinner & stayed all afternoon & Oscar took them back in the evening. Karsten was out a little while in the evening. Oscar & I went to church, the young people had charge of the meeting. [Rev. Alexander v.] Hoiriis was to conference in Viborg, S.D.

Sept. 18 – To-day it rained hard all day. We couldn't hardly go outside. It was the first hard rain we had since the bridge was put in. It washed a lot of dirt away. The old bridge is there yet.

Sun. Sept. 21 – It rained hard last night. Oscar went down to Walnut to get Mabel & Walter & kids. Walter was going up north to rent a farm. [80] Mabel stayed home till Saturday. Mr. & Mrs. Sahl came up here in the afternoon a while. Oscar took Walt to the train Monday morning the 22nd. Walt rented 141 acres north of Bisgards. $1200 in rent. We went to town Monday afternoon, Mabel & Ma got their new winter hats. Mabel's hat had blue on top of the crown. We got Melvin's & Lela's pictures taken.

**Lela and Melvin Larsen – 1919
(Photo by Morehouse.)**

Page 126 – 1919

Oscar started to fall plow Wed the Sept 24th on the 12 acres.

Sept. 29 – To-day it is cloudy. Oscar is plowing. Roy Brodersen flew over here in his airplane. He flew southeast from here. He flew to Elk Horn a few days ago.

Oct. 7 – Elmer Arentsen took Uncle Andrew [81] & his wife up to see us to-day. Elmer helped Oscar build our machine shed. In the

---

[80] The farm was in Palo Alto County, northwest of Emmetsburg, Iowa, near Ruthven.
[81] Mrs. Arentsen was Mary Christensen, sister to Andrew Christensen, A brother, Lars Peter Christensen, was married to Martine's sister,

evening we went out to the church for the last homecoming for the soldier boys. The boys were not all there. They had a program and server supper. There was a large crowd. It was a very nice evening.

Page 127 – 1919

Oct. 18 – To-day it is good weather but kinda hot. Oscar picked 2 loads of corn. He stated to pick to-day the 20 acres.

Oct. 19 – Oscar & I went to church & Sunday School. To-day Arentsen's came with us home for dinner. It rained after dinner so they had to go home. Louis was also here for dinner.

Oct. 22 – They are going to have a surprise on [Rev. Alexander V.] Hoiriis' to-night.

Oct. 25 – To-day it is sleeting a little. Oscar picked 8 rows in the forenoon & Mama helped him pick 9 rows of corn in the afternoon. I had such terrible bad cold all day. Oscar went to town last night. He got me a gray sweater.

Oct. 26 – It is cold and a little cloudy. Ma & Oscar went to church to-day. I stayed alone home. [Rev. Alexander V.] Hoiriis will preach his last sermon to-day. They will then leave for Westbrook, Minn to be there by Nov. 1. They left in their Ford, Oct 29 for Alta about 3 o'clock in the afternoon, then from there to Westbrook Minn.

Page 128 – 1919

Oct. 24 – To-day Harold W. Findlay & Olo Pearl Dent surprised their many friends by getting married at the Methodist parsonage by Rev. G. T. Roberts. They were accompanied by Arlene

Ottomine. Andrew was not an Uncle to Martha, but Uncle (Lars) Peter's brother.

Denton & George Gregory. Mrs. W. H. Mayne gave a shower for the bride the 25th. About 35 were present.

Oct. 15 – Miss Floy Allen & Mr. Harry Sorensen went to Omaha & were married to-day.

Oct. 30 – To-day Miss Carrie Norgaard & Ora Argotsinger were married at the home of Rev. J[ulius] A. Jensen.

Oct. 17 – Tina Fredricksen was married to Morten Normolle in Denmark to-day. She had been in America about 14 years and then went to Denmark & was married.

Nov. 2 – To-day it is a little cold. We went down to Walnut. Mabel & family has moved in another house west of the M. E. Church & a little south. It is the third house they have lived in Walnut. They will just live there 2 months & then move up to Emmetsburg.

Page 129 – 1919

Nov. 4 – To-day we finished picking the 20 acres. We got the crib full to the top about 800 bu.

Nov. 11 – To-day it is a little cloudy but not very cold. We picked 19 rows of corn below the grove. It is white corn. Roy Brodersen flew over here in his areoplane, to Atlantic to a celebration. We saw him come back too. We saw an aroplane fly over town. We saw him light 5 times. I guess it was Emil Nelson.

Nov. 12 – To-day it has been awful cold. It was 3 above zero. It snowed some last night. We had the milk cows in the barn last night. We went out to pick this morning about 7 o'clock. We was about the only team out. We picked 18 rows to-day. We have the big wire cribbing full.

Nov. 17 – To-day we finished picking corn. We picked 35 acres. We got 2 big wire cribbing full besides the big crib. About 1400 bu.

Page 130 – 1919

Nov. 23 – To-day we went to church. When we got there we saw Uncle Pete [82] with Arentsens. He had come to Walnut the day before & surprised them. We all had our picture taken.

Nov. 24 – To-day Ma & Oscar went to town. They bo't a new rocking chair with upholstery. We were over to Mike's to-night, the first time in the new house. They have Delco light.

Nov. 27 – To-day it is snowing a little and it is kinda cold. It snowed hard last night & blowed. We have just had all our stock in 2 nights. It is Thanksgiving Day. Oscar has started down to Walnut to get Mabel & family. Lela is 2 yrs old to-day. They stayed overnight. To-day the 28th Oscar took them home about noon. It has been snowing all day.

Dec. 1 – To-day it is awful cold. Oscar & I went to town. I got that false tooth put in, that I broke off.

Dec. 2 – To-day Oscar & I hauled straw & then Uncle Pete & Mrs. Arentsen came up here for dinner. They stayed all day. Mr. & Mrs. Sahl & Thorvald came up awhile in the afternoon & Louis came also.

Page 131 -1919

Dec. 6 – To-day Uncle Pete, Stella & Eddie [Arentsen] went to town in the bobsled. Oscar went with them. Uncle Pete stayed

---

[82] Uncle Pete was possibly Martine's brother, Christen Peter Nelsen. But it is more likely he was (Lars) Peter Christensen, Martine's brother-in-law, and Mrs. Arentsen's brother.

here overnight when they came from town. The trees was full of
frost this morning, Sun. Dec. 7. Oscar took Uncle Pete down to
Arentsen's with Babe & Goldie on the bobsled. Ma & I was
home all day.

Dec. 9 – To-day it is cold & lots of snow. It snowed & drifted all
day yesterday & all night. Oscar went up to Soren Jensen's sale,
horseback. The school house hill is drifted full. They have to
drive in the field. We are washing to-day.

Dec. 12 – To-day it is cold. It is Melvin's 5th birthday. There is
snow on the ground. It is W. C. Sorensen's sale.

Dec. 21 – To-day it is quite cold. Oscar & I went to church in the
bobsled. [Rev. Niel S.] Lawdahl spoke . We drove Babe &
Goldie.

Dec. 22 – We went to town in the bobsled, Babe & Goldie. I got
4 teeth filled to-day.

Page 132 - 1919

Dec. 25 – To-day is Xmas Day. We have been alone home all
day. It hasn't been so very cold. The wind is in the south. I got
my Kodak album from Ma, crepe de chine hkch from Chris &
Emma, 2 postal cards.

1920

Jan. 1 – To-day it is quite cold. We were out to the church to-day. It was 50 yrs ago (1870 – 1920) since it was organized. There was quite a few people there. They came nearly all in sleds. There was 2 cars out there too. They served dinner & supper. There was 6 people left that was there when it was organized. There were 2 out there to-day. They were Mrs. Michael Hansen & Jens Rold. Mr. Michael Hansen was not able to come up there, but he was also one of them. And Peter Rold was one of them. He lives in Calif. Mrs. Marinus Christensen was also one of them. Rev. P. H. Dam was the first preacher out there. They were presented each with a boquet of flowers.

Jan. 2 – To-day it is nice weather, a little snow on the ground. We shelled corn. [Above it states: Sam M. shelled it.] The white corn in the wire cribs. We sold 318 bu to Ralph Miller.

Page 133 – 1920

Jan. 7 – It is blowing to-day & a little cold. Ivan age 20 & Bernice age 19 was married in town to-day. Rev. Roberts married them. There were 40 boys over in the evening to chivarie them.

Jan. 9 – This morning Mabel & Melvin & Lela came on the train from Walnut. Oscar went in after them in the car. They had all their household goods shipped to Osgood, Ia. [83] The goods left Walnut Jan 10 Sat.

Jan. 12 – Walter came out here and went on the train to Emmetsburg to get the goods out of the car & out to the place.

---

[83] Osgood was north of Emmetsburg on the west branch of the Des Moines River and closer to their farm than Emmetsburg.

Jan. 13th - A baby girl was born to Mr. & Mrs. James Andersen. They have 3 boys & 1 girl now.

Jan. 17 – To-day Mabel & Lela & Oscar went to town. Mabel went in to see Stena Sahl. They went in the car.

Jan. 19 – It is cold to-day. Oscar took Mabel, Melvin & Lela in to the 9 o'clock train. They have been here over 1 wk. They are going to Ruthven. Walter went up there a week ago. They are going up on a 141 acre farm.

Page 134 – 1920

Jan. 22 – To-day it is cold & cloudy. We went out to Bergs a little while. Mrs. Berg had just come home from Chicago the 18th Sunday. She was down there 3 wks. We went thru town coming home. Mabel works by Mary Jane Wyland, over Madsen store. She gave me a silver teaspoon, the first one I ever had.

Jan. 23 – To-day it is snowing some. Oscar took that sulky plow in to send it up to Ruthven. Walter will get it there & take it home. Mabel is 26 years old to-day.

Jan. 27 – To-day it is quite cold. Oscar took in 6 spring pigs. He got $14.40 a lb. They weighed 183 lbs.

Jan. 28 – A baby boy was born to Mr. & Mrs. Paul Kemp to-day. He was named Howard Edwin. It weighed 8 ½ lbs.

Jan. 30 – Twin boys were born to Mr. & Mrs. Alvin Christensen this morning.

Jan. 31 – To-day it has been damp & cloudy. Oscar & I have been chopping trees down northeast of the house along Bamsey's fence.

Feb. 3 – It is icy all over & now it is snowing this afternoon. Mrs. Clarence Johnson passed away this morning. She fist had the flu & then pneumonia. She died in their garage.

Page 135 - 1920

Feb. 5 – It snowed & rained last night & there is about 5 in of snow on the ground. Mrs. Clarence Johnson is buried to-day. The funeral was 10 o'clock at Dahlof's her folks. She was born July 22, 1884.

Feb. 14 – It is cold to-day. It is zero. Mrs. Andrew Klitgard died yesterday. I am going to sew on Lela [Larsen]'s dark blue spring coat to-day.

Feb. 11 – Roy Reinhart & Emma Johnson was married at the Lutheran parsonage to-day.

Feb. 23 – To-day I finished Lela's blue spring coat. It has been cold & cloudy all day. Clarence Johnson had his sale to-day. He made about $65.00. We got 17 eggs to-day.

Feb. 26 – It is cold to-day. It froze hard last night but it is clear to-day. Oscar is 20 yrs old to-day. It warmed up this afternoon. Oscar & I chopped some apple trees down to-day. We are getting up a wood pile north of the house.

Mar. 1 – We went to town in the car to-day. The roads are dry some places. It is nice weather overhead. I got some plaid gingham for an apron. I was up visiting Mabel Berg where she works at Mary Jane Wyland.

Page 136 – 1920

Mar. 3 – To-day it is raining. The snow is nearly all gone. There is going to be Ladies Aid down to Arentsen's tomorrow.

Mar. 4 – It has drifted & cold all day. We got 24 eggs to-day. Mabel Andersen & Thorvald Andersen were married at the bride's mother. She was 17 yrs old.

Mar. 5 – The Basket Store opened on the east side in Harlan to-day.

Mar. 6 – A baby girl was born to Mr. & Mrs. M. G. Christensen to-day. It's wgt. 6 ½ lbs. It has been named Ileen Ann.

Mar. 11 – It thundered & lightninged last night & rained, the first time this spring. It is nice weather to-day. The snow is all gone, all but a little on the north side of buildings.

Mar. 12 – This morning Walter's father [84] died of heart failure. He died down by Jim's in Walnut. He was buried Sunday, Mar. 14 in Walnut Cemetery. Willis & Walter came down for the funeral.

Mar. 16 – Yesterday it blowed terrible all day & also last night. Willis & Walter came here last night from Adam Sorensen's. Oscar took them in to the train this morning. The roads are pretty good.

Page 137 – 1920

Mar. 18 – To-day Ethel Christensen & Edwin Larsen were married.

---

[84] Nels Peter Larsen, Aug. 22, 1849 – Mar. 12, 1920, was buried in the Layton Township (Walnut) Cemetery according to Find-A-Grave Memorial # 114961609.

Mar. 22 – To-day we were to funeral John Edwards [85] was buried. He died at the Methodist hospital in Omaha Friday night the 19th. The church was full of people. He was 21 yrs. old.

Mar. 23 – Oscar took in the last 5 of our spring pigs average 166 lbs. I planted my sweat peas to-day. It is blowing to-day.

Mar. 27 – This afternoon Old Mrs. Soren Knudson [86] was buried. She died the 23rd at C. G. Sorensen's. [Rev. Julius] A. Jensen said the funeral sermon. She was 86 yrs old.

Mar. 31 – To-day Oscar started to disc the 20 acres kitter in the north forty. It is blowing hard & is warm to-day. We have been cleaning the house up and baking cakes & cookies for the Ladies Aid to-morrow. It looks like rain. The grass is starting to look green.

April 1 – To-day it is cold & snow on the ground. It is Easter Sunday. We are home to-day. We have 4 little pigs. Mabel Berg & Frank Heilesen was here in the afternoon. Mabel gave me a silver teaspoon.

April 4 – To-day it is cold & snow on the ground. It is Easter Sunday. We are home to-day. We have 4 little pigs. Mabel Berg & Frank Heilesen was here in the afternoon. Mabel gave me a silver teaspoon.

Page 138 – 1920

Apr. 2 – I got my black straw hat trimmed with blue straw around the edge & also a flower.

---

[85] John Edwards, 1899 – 1920, was buried at Cuppy's Grove according to Find-A-Grave Memorial # 98489860.
[86] Ann Knudsen, Feb. 8, 1834 – Mar. 25, 1920, was buried at the Harlan Cemetery according to Find-A-Grave Memorial # 28170345.

Apr. 7 – Oscar started to seed to-day. The 10 acres in north forty. I planted onion seeds & onion sets, radishes & lettuce. It is nice weather to-day.

Apr. 8 – It is warm weather to-day. Oscar finished seeding 10 acres oats. I am raking the yard to-day. We have 2 hens setting.

Apr. 11 – To-day it rained in the forenoon, and snowed in the afternoon. It is about 2 inches of snow on the ground. To-morrow morning I was going to go with Moder & Marie [87] up north if the weather had been nice. Harry Hendricksen & his wife has been over here on Clarence Johnson's place about a wk.

Apr. 13 – This morning on the 9 o'clock train, Marie & Moder & I left for Ruthven. We stayed up there till the 19th. We had a good time.

Apr. 23 – It is raining to-day & a little chilly. Oscar started this forenoon with the Grand DeTour sulky. We only have 8 little chickens and 20 little pigs.

Page 139 – 1920

April 29 – It is cloudy & chilly to-day. We have 23 little pigs & 23 little chickens. Oscar will finish plowing the 10 acres in the north forty.

April 27 – We were in town to-day. Mama got her new spring hat to-day with the wheat, maline, & black velvet ribbon on. Ma got goods for gingham dress. It is tan plaid and I got pink plaid 55¢ a yd.

---

[87] It is likely that Moder (Danish for Mother) was not Martha's grandmother, but instead Mabel's mother-in-law, Beathe Larsen. Marie would have been Marie Larsen, wife to Walter's brother, Jim Larsen. Both were from Walnut.

May 2 – It is nice weather to-day. [Rev.] Andrew [Christophersen] spoke in our church to-day. We went out there for Sunday school We had the vetenenary out for that white faced heifer. We went to church in the evening.

May 3 – It is windy & chilly to-day. We went up to see Jennie. We got some eggs exchanged. Oscar finished plowing to-day.

May 5 – To-day it is nice warm weather. We cleaned Ma's and my bedroom & had the rug out. My peas & sweat peas are just starting to come up. We are going out to the "Hard Times" social out by the "parsonage" to-night. We have to wear our old clothes.

May 16 – It is cold to-day & it rained some. We went to church. They had fire in the furnace. A. Danielson [88] spoke out there. We have 57 little chickens.

Page 140 – 1920

May 18 – It is warm & windy to-day. I cleaned the kitchen & varnished some chairs. Oscars going to start to plant the 7 acres this afternoon. That is all he has left. The pansys are in bloom & the apple & cherry trees are in bloom. I sowed some flower seeds yesterday.

---

[88] Rev. Alfred Danielson served Cuppy's Grove from 1920 to 1923.

Keldgord garden - 1926 (family photo)

May 20 – It is nice weather to-day. To-night we went down to John Nelson's, the church had a surprise on Nellie in honor of her approaching marriage. They gave her a set of silverware. We had ice cream & cookies.

May 23 – It rained hard last night but we went to church. The roads were dry when church was out. We were invited down to Arentsens' for dinner. Martha Hansen & Edwin Nelson were down there also. Arentsens had 400 chickens & 16 goslings.

May 24 – It is fine weather to-day. We washed & went to town in the afternoon. & got my blue figured voile & my pink plaid gingham dress. Mrs. Wilson made them.

May 25 – We can almost row our 13 acres now.

May 30 – It is nice weather to-day. Oscar & I went to church. Our preacher Mr. Danielson was married the 25th. It was the last Sunday that Nellie would be in our church for a while.

Page 141 – 1920

May 31 – Oscar started to plow corn to-day. I planted cucumbers in the 13 acres to-day.

June 11 – A baby girl was born to-day to Mr. & Mrs. Martin Arentsen. Her name is Eleanor Marie.

June 12 – A baby boy was born to-day to Mr. & Mrs. Russel Christensen. Wgt 8 lbs name Eugene.

June 13 – It has been hot to-day. We have been out to "Children's Day" program at out church. It was a good program. Mr. & Mrs. Danielson sang a duet. In the evening we went to Harlan to program.

June 14 – Oscar finished crossing the corn to-day, all but a few rows. The roses are just about in bloom.

June 14 – Dena Christensen & John Gasner were married in Oakland.

June 3 – This evening Nellie Nelson & Niel Berg was married by her uncle [Rev.] Jacob Vinding. Just their relatives were present. She wore a white silk dress. In about a wk they drove out to Okko Nebr in their Ford. Her folks gave her a Hallet & Davis piano. Oscar was with a crowd & chivaried them.

June 28 – To-day Oscar started to lay by the corn. We have 30 acres.

Page 142 – 1920

July 1 – To-day it rained this morning & cleared up at noon & about 5 o'clock it rained hard again. Our raspberries are getting ripe.

July 2 – I picked 7 qts of raspberries to-day. We canned 6 qts.

July 4 – I stayed over night with Mabel Berg last night & to-day. We went down to Lake Wanawa & Krug Park [an amusement park] Omaha. Frank & Mabel & Howard & I. We sailed across

Lake Manawa in a motor boat. We was on a Roly Polys in Krug park. It was hot & dusty down there. We got home about half past ten.

July 11 – It is real nice weather to-day. We was out by Bergs for dinner. Mabel was home. Mabel & I & Gordon & Oscar drove up to Mike's a little while & heard their victrola. "Silvertone".

July 11 – We have picked about 30 quts of raspberries this year. We have canned about 25 quts.

July 14 – To-day it is nice weather. The wind is in the northeast. Oscar is over by Findlay's. They are cutting oats this forenoon & going to make hay this afternoon. Our tomatoes plants have little tomatoes on them. We have canned 8 quts of beets. We canned 3 quts of our own cherries.

Page 143 – 1920

July 15 - To-day is a fine day. Oscar is mowing our ten acres this afternoon. Harold is going to help mow it. Forest is going to cut his oats this afternoon.

July 17 – To-day is nice weather. We got our hay put up to-day. We got a few loads in yesterday. The hay was cured fine, all but a few loads.

July 18 – It is nice weather to-day. We went to church. J. C. Lunn preached to-day because Danielson is in Minneapolis. He has been sick the last while, but he will be back by the 25th.

July 26 – To-day we got thru cutting oats. We had 18 acres.

Aug 7 – It is hot to-day. Oscar is over by Ivan's threshing to-day. We threshed yesterday. They started about 11 o'clock and we had them for dinner. They got thru about 5 o'clock. We got 639 bu of oats. We had 14 men.

Aug 7 – We have canned 7 quts of ripe cucumbers already & we will have a lot more. I have them planted in the twelve acres. We have canned 3 ½ quts of blackberries this summer & made a lot of jell & jam.

Aug. 1 – Last Sunday Mabel Berg & Carsten was here, but Mabel has been here since the 27th of July. That day Ma & Oscar left for a visit up by Mabel. They just stayed till the 31st. We took pictures that Sun afternoon.

Page 144 – 1920

Aug. 17 – It is warm to-day. Oscar fixed a lane for the cows to go over in the 10 acres of meadow. The pasture is so dry. Roy's are threshing to-day. Hans Jensen is running his tractor with a separator. John Nelson & others have bot in partnership. We made Apple butter yesterday. We have canned about 80 qt.

Aug. 19 – It has been raining nearly all day. It was a nice rain, the first rain for 6 wks. The pastures were drying up and the tomatoes were drying. We have canned about 15 quts of cucumber. We made some wild grape jell to-day. Mr. and Mrs. Marinus Christensen were her a little while towards evening yesterday. Oscar went to Fair yesterday. The Brundige Shows was down there.

Aug. 24 – To-day Rev. Alfred Danielson was ordained. The exam started at 1:30 till 3 o'clock and then we had lunch and then the ordination started at 4 o'clock. There were old Rev.[W. J.] Andreasen, [Rev. Rasmus] Christensen, D. D. Downs, [Rev.] S. C. Sonnickson, [Rev. Julius] A. Jensen, [Rev.] Ralph Jensen & J. C. Lunn & then Danielson. They each gave a talk. [Rev.] Ralph Jensen give the ordination prayer.

Page 145 – 1920

Sept. 5 – It is nice weather to-day. We were home. Bergs & Grace & Georgine were here for dinner & for lunch. Mike was working. Mabel & Frank didn't come. We went to church in the evening.

Sept. 6 – To-day is nice weather. Oscar is plowing the 8 acres of stubble. We canned some snow apples to-day. We have canned 25 quts of cucumbers this year & 14 quts of beets and 80 quts of fruit.

Sept. 11 – It is real nice weather to-day. We canned plum butter & yellow tomatoes. We made pumpkin pie too.

Sept. 12 – We are going to church to-day. Dr. Foley of Minneapolis is going to speak. He had spoke every night & afternoon during the week. It has been Bible Conference.

Sept. 16 –To-day is fine weather. We went to Walnut this afternoon. We havn't been down there since Mabel moved away. Madsen Bros were selling out. We bo't a few things.

Sept. 17 – This afternoon we went to town & I went out to Martin & Vina [Arentsen]. It was the first time I had seen the baby. Eileen is now 3 yrs. old and the baby is 3 mos.

Page 146 – 1920

Sept. 17 – It is just fine weather to-day. Oscar picked seed corn & I canned a few yellow tomatoes & we bro't some pumpkins & cucumbers home from the field. We have canned 30 quts of cucumbers besides those to-day.

Sept. 21 – To-day it is warm and windy. Mama & Oscar went to town to-day. They took in 9 spring roosters and got $9.18 for them. They weighed a little more than 4 lbs a pc. Eggs are 46¢ a doz to-day, butter 55¢, sugar 20¢. Oscar got his new dress shirt with silk stripes $6.30.

Sept. 4 – To-day a 7 lb boy was born to cousin Martin [Christensen] & wife. [89] His name is William Lars.

Oct. 2 – We were in town to-day. I got my black velvet hat with feathers around the crown.

Oct. 3 – To-day is fine weather. We went to church and was down by Arentsen's for dinner.

Oct. 5 – To-day is very nice weather. We cleaned Mama's & my bedroom and we made 5 quts of pickalily. [A type of relish.]

Oct. 2 – To-day E. A. Hamelbrath & Rose Ruska were married at the Lutheran parsonage. They have rooms by Mrs. Pence Miller.

Page 147 – 1920

Oct. 10 – It is nice weather to-day. It isn't a bit cold. We went to church in the forenoon. Rev. A. Danielson spoke in the Norwegian language. R. J. Rasmussen were out there. They came along with us home for dinner.

Oct. 13 – It is warm & windy to-day. We piled some wood on that pile northeast of the house this forenoon. This afternoon Oscar& I picked five rows of corn in the 12 acres. The first load this fall. It is laying down so bad. It is hard to follow the rows.

Oct. 20 – To-day is cloudy and it is warm. We picked 18 rows to-day. We have picked about 7 acres out of the 12 acres. To-day is the 21st. Oscar went to town to get some potatoes on the track. He got 5 bu of white potatoes at $1.15 a bu.

Oct. 24 – It froze a little last night but the sun is shining bright. Oscar & I went to church. Mama had such a bad cold she

---

[89] This was confirmed in California Birth Index.

couldn't go along. There was baptism by A. Danielson to-day. They were Oscar, Chester V., Arlo N., Clifford T, Cliff S, Mabel Sorensen & Lulu Troll.

Oct. 23 – A baby girl was born to Mr. & Mrs. Thorvald Andersen to-day. Her name is Ione Muriel.

Oct. 31 – It is raining to-day, Sunday. We have picked corn 2 wks. We have picked the 12 acres & almost thru with the 10 acres. We got our crib nearly full.

Page 148 – 1920

Nov. 2 – To-day is nice weather but yesterday was a cold day. It snowed a little and it froze hard last night. We put up our little heater to-day. We picked 9 rows of the ten acres this afternoon. We will finish that piece to-morrow.

Nov. 6 – To-day it rained nearly all day. We have only about 37 rows of corn left in the 7 acres. We have picked 22 acres. Oscar drove to town to-day in the little buggy with Doll & Babe. We got 6 eggs to-day.

Nov. 8 – Twins, a boy & a girl, was born to Mr. & Mrs. Martin Grann to-day. They weighed each 6 lbs.

Nov. 11 – To-day it is cold. It froze hard last night. We just had to milk cows in the barn last night. It has been blowing from the northwest. We picked the last 18 rows of the 7 acres. We are thru picking thirty acres. We got our crib full & 300 bu in the wire cribbing.

Nov. 12 - To-day it is cold. We went to town in the car, I got my blue wool poplin goods to-day. Nora Jorgens is going to make it.

The first part of August the church got new song books. "The Popular Hymnal".

Nov. 19 – It is nice weather to-day. We cleaned the kitchen and Oscar is picking the 3rd day for Forrest [Findlay].

Nov. 20 – It has been real nice weather to-day. Oscar finished picking for Forrest to-day. He picked around 200 bu and got $22.25.

Nov. 21 – Louis Berg was here this evening. We all went to Harlan church and he stayed her over night. He will leave for Calif. one of the days.

Nov. 23 – To-day it is cloudy & chilly. Oscar hauled 1800 lbs of hard coal. He hauled 900 lbs. a few weeks ago and tomorrow he will haul the rest.

Nov. 29 – To-day was Sahl's sale. It rained nearly all forenoon. They had free lunch at noon and the sale started at 1 o'clock. Corn sold for 42¢ a bu, hogs sold for $12 a piece. The roads were terrible muddy, one horse sold for $125, one cow for over $100.

Dec. 9 – It has been cloudy & damp to-day. We went to town to get my wool poplin dress trimmed with military braid. Nora Jorgensen made it for $5.

Dec. 9 – To-day Oscar went up to Gillett's to get the hay loader. He bo't on their sale the 30th of Nov. He got the dump rake the other day.

Dec. 16 – To-day it blowed hard. The roads are fine. We havn't had a snow yet this year. Minnie & Doris Ann and Jennie were up here a little while this afternoon. I am home to-day.

An 8 lb girl was born to Mr. & Mrs. Harry Hendricksen this morning. Her name is Margaret Elaine.

Page 150 – 1920

Dec. 19 - To-day has been cold and cloudy most of the day. It was almost down to zero this morning. Mama & Oscar went to church to-day. I had a bad cold and I have been hoarse for a few days. We got 17 eggs to-day. The roads are fine now. It snowed a little last night.

Dec. 20 – To-day Sahl's moved to town. Oscar hauled a load in the hayrack.

Dec. 21 - To-day the ground is covered with snow. It sleeted & snowed & blowed from the east last night. Oscar went up to Ed Anthony's to get our Litchfield spreader. He bo't it on the sale for $55.

Dec. 22 – A nine lb boy was born to Mr. & Mrs. Harold Findlay to-day. His name is James Riley.

Dec. 29 – Stella A. [Arentsen] & Geo Mikkelsen were married to-day at Rev. J[ulius] A. Jensen's to-day.

Dec. 27 – It is terrible cold to-day. Oscar took in 6 of our spring pigs. He got $8.50.

Dec. 28 - To-day Sam M. sawed out big wood pile, northeast of the house. Forest & Harold helped saw it.

1921

Jan. 2, 1921 – We were all to church to-day. The roads was not very good. We were at Anton Simmonsen's for dinner. Oscar and Henry went skating in the afternoon. We went over to see Old Mrs. Mike Hansen. She is in bed most of the time.

Jan. 4 – We went to town in the car. The roads were muddy. We visited Soren Jensen's the first time in town. Oscar bo't 4 new split dorf plugs the second set of split dorf & new half wind shield. [Apparently for the Ford car.]

Page 151 – 1921

Jan. 12 – It is nice weather to-day. We went out to Bergs for Dinner in the car. The roads were good.

Jan. 13 – To-day it snowed all day. At 12 o'clock Mabel Berg and Frank Heileson were married at Rev. J[ulius] A. Jensen's. They left immediately for Omaha & also Dunlap to visit Mike Rath & wife.

Mrs. Martin C. & Grace & Ileen were over here this afternoon. Jan. 13.

Jan. 18 - It is windy & cold to-day. Ma and Oscar went to town to get Mr. & Mrs. Chris Johnson and Otellie from Shell Lake Wis. They staid overnight and took them in town the next day. They were going to leave on the 3 o'clock train to Laurens.

Jan. 22 – A 6 lb boy was born to Mr. & Mrs. Ivan E. Christensen to-day. It has been named Kenneth Kemp.

Jan. 28 – We had a missionary program at out church to-night It was real good. They took up a collection of $20.00 for a missionary in Africa.

Feb. 4 – A 6 ½ lb boy was born to Mr. & Mrs. Ed Andersen to-day.

Feb. 4 – We went to town to-day. Oscar got his new chocolate brown suit with a belt on for $50 at Paulk & Hansen's.

Feb. 6 – To-day is Sunday. We have been home alone all day. It had snowed and drifted all day. The cows have been in the barn all day. Yesterday the sun was so warm & it was melting.

Page 152 – 1921

Feb. 12 – We were over to Martin C. last night. We walked over. We got 26 eggs to-day. To-day we were in town. I got a wisdom tooth pulled and 2 teeth filled. We drove the car, but the roads were pretty bad.

Feb. 12 – A 11 ¼ baby girl was born to Mr. & Mrs. Paul Kemp to-day. She is named Arla May.

Feb. 3 – To-day Sarah Anderson and Jacob Jorgensen were married at the brides home in Harlan by Rev. J[ulius] A. Jensen.

Feb. 15 – To-day it is nice weather, not a bit cold. The snow is all gone. The river is bank full. We lost that red milk cow to-day. She was fresh yesterday. She was 5 yrs.

Oscar is helping Harold saw wood to-day.

Feb. 16 – It is cold and windy to-day. Sam Shelled 300 bu out of the crib. We sold 200 bu to Luke Heflin at 45¢ a bu.

Feb. 20 – It is chilly to-day. The wind is blowing from the south. We went to church. [Rev. Martin] A. Wesgard is here, beginning with a series of meetings for about 2 wks.

Feb. 28 – It is warm weather to-day. We washed and Oscar hauled hogs for Forrest. We got 37 eggs to-day. We went to church to-night. The roads are just fine. Eddie Arentsen was pretty sick to-day.

March 3 – It is fine weather to-day. We went to church to-night & Mrs. Martin Christensen went with us.

Page 153 – 1921

Mar. 2 – Evelyn Vinding & Leslie Edwards were married at 6:30 to-night. At her home by Rev. A. Danielson.

Mar. 6 – We went to church to-day and also in the evening. It was the last meeting for [Rev. Martin] A. Wesgard for 2 wks. There were 7 converted.

Mar. 10 – It is windy to-day. Oscar started to plow sod behind the grove. I ironed to-day & trimmed raspberry bushes.

Mar. 11 – We got 50 eggs to-day.

Mar. 14 – R. J. Rasmussen [90] died to-day at his home near Jacksonville. He was 84 yrs. The funeral is going to be held the 17th at 12 o'clock at the home & 1 o'clock at the Danish Church at Harlan.

Mar. 24 – Hans Rasmussen brot the red bull up. We paid $60 for him.

Mar. 30 – Christian Rold & Esther Larsen were married this evening at the brides home in Harlan.

Mar. 31 – Octave Nelson & Myrtle Rold were married this evening at the brides home. Oscar went to the chivari. There was a large crowd.

---

[90] Rasmus J. Rasmussen, Sept. 18, 1834 – Mar. 14, 1921, was buried in the Jacksonville Cemetery according to Find-A-Grave Memorial # 114117524.

April 3 – It is blowing hard to-day & it is so dusty in the air. We were to church and over to Andrew Christensen for dinner.

April 6 – It rained two hard showers to-day. We planted potatoes below the grove. We have 19 little chickens & 1 hen hatching to-day. We have 20 little pigs.

Page 154 – 1921

Apr. 9 - It is cold and snowing some to-day. We went down to Walnut to get Aunt Florence [Nelson] & Eleanor. They came from La Crosse. We went to church Sunday and to John Vinding's for dinner and to Harlan church in the evening. Monday evening the 11th we were down to Arentsen's for supper. Aunt Florence & Eleanor staid there over night. The next day Arentsens took her to Avoca.

Apr. 14 – I planted tomato seed out in the garden to-day. We have 30 little chickens & 9 hens setting.

Apr. 16 – It snowed & froze some last night. The plum trees are in bloom.

Apr. 21 – To-day is a little cloudy. We papered the kitchen. It is plain paper with a cut out border.

Apr. 24 – Oscar & I went to Sunday School to-day. Chris Petersens were here from Jacksonville.

Apr. 25 – To-day I kalsomined the ceiling in Mama's room & papered the walls.

Apr. 26 – To-day we got a red cow of of Hans Rasmussen. We traded for our white faced heifer.

May 3 – To-day is fine weather. I ironed this forenoon & cleaned the front room this afternoon. It froze some last night. Minnie & Doris Ann were up here to-day. We have 129 little chickens.

Page 155 – 1921

May 6 – A 10 lb girl was born to Mr. & Mrs. Forest Findlay to-day. Her name is Betty Jean.

May. 7 – A baby boy was born to Rev. & Mrs. A. Danielson to-day.

May 21 – To-day has been hot. We went out to cemetery to fix the graves. We went down to look at the dredge. It is west of Michael Hansen.

May 25 – We bo't our set of asbestos sad irons to-day of Hansen Hardware store for $3.50.

May 30 – It has rained 2 or 3 showers to-day. I put out about 150 red & yellow tomato plants to-day. Oscar has plowed 21 acres of corn the first time.

June 5 – It is fine weather. It has been warm to-day. We went out this afternoon to Rally in Merrill's Grove. They had a nice program. We went out to our church in the evening. [Rev.] Thomas Hansen of Des Moines spoke.

June 6 – It is nice weather. Oscar started to cross the corn to-day. I made rhubarb jell to-day. I have put out around 250 tomatoe plants this spring.

June 18 – It has been awfull warm to-day. Oscar is laying by the corn. I picked 2 quts of raspberries to-day. The first picking. We had the first spring chicken & new peas.

June 24 – I picked 10 qts of raspberries to-day. We sold 8 qts to Frank & Mabel. Oscar is mowing hay in the north forty. We are going to make hay this afternoon. Elmer Steele is helping us. We have new beans & a spring chicken for dinner.

Page 156 - 1921

June 29 – We finished putting up hay to-day. We got 29 loads of 10 acres. The barn is full. We exchanged with Elmer Steele. I made some raspberry jam to-day.

July 4 – It has been warm to-day. It rained hard last night. Mama & I was home all day. Oscar was out to the parsonage in the afternoon.

July 11 – To-day Pete Greve came up here to cut our grain. He finished the next day.

July 12 – We started to pick blackberries to-day. I picked 10 qts. They are 35¢ a qts this year.

July 24 – It is fine weather to-day. We have picked over 100 qts of blackberries this year. We have sold 87 qts. We pick around 30 qts at every picking. They have started to thresh around here now.

Aug. 2 – It is nice weather to-day. We canned our first yellow tomatoes to-day and canned some green cucumbers. We are going to pick the last blackberries to-morrow. We have picked 150 qts and sold 102 qts. We have a lot of cucumbers this year.

Page 157 – 1921

Aug. 7 – Oscar threshed by Luka's yesterday. Oscar went to Sunday School to-day. We all went out to George & Stella this afternoon. Our red & yellow tomatoes are getting ripe. We have canned 19qts of green cucumbers & about 16 qts of ripe ones. We raised a cucumber that was 13 in. long & 11 circumference.

Aug. 6 – About noon to-day Eddie Hollenbeck [91] & a friend stopped here a while. They are driving in a Ford from New York to Calif. We didn't hardly know him. His wife and child are in New York.

Aug. 13 – We threshed this afternoon. We had 2 men for supper. They got thru about 5:30 o'clock. We have canned some yellow tomato preserves this year.

Aug. 23 – There was a S.S. picnic at the park, back of the parsonage. It rained in the forenoon but we went out in the afternoon. They had a good program. Merrill's Grove SS got the banner. It was embroidered by Neva Rold.

Aug. 26 – To-day I went with Pete Hansen's up to Mabel. We started 11 o'clock from Manning and got up there 6 o'clock. I stayed up there 3 wks till Sept 15. I went with Bisgaards to Lost Island Lake Sept 11th to a S.S. picnic. I came home Thurs the 15th on the 8:31 train.

[91] Eddie Hollenbeck was Martha's cousin, son of Jacob Keldgord's sister, Karen Marie (Mary) Hollenbeck.

1920s Picnic (family photo)

Page 157 – 1921

Sept. 23 - A 11 ½ lb boy was born to Ellis & Blanche Gearhart to-day. Name Lynn Alden.

Sept. 27 – We were in town to-day. I got my new black, lace kid shoes. $7.00.

Oct. 1 – Soren Jensen [92] died at his home in Harlan to-day and was buried the 5th. We were in to the funeral.

Oct. 8 – To-day is fine weather. We started to pick the 12 acres. We picked 70 bu. the corn is sure dry.

Oct. 15 – This afternoon we finished picking the 12 acres. It aveg. 45 bu to the acre. We put most of it in the wire cribbing. It has been warm to-day.

Oct. 14 – An 8 lb baby boy was born to Mr. & Mrs. Geo Mikkelsen to-day. His name is Harold Bernard.

---

[92] Soren C. Jensen, 1856 – 1921, was buried in the Harlan Cemetery according to Find-A-Grave Memorial # 38789107.

Nov. 8 – To-day it is snowing. The ground is white. It sure is cold. To-day is the 9th. We picked 2 loads and we have 9 short rows left. We picked 1675 bu corn.

Nov. 10 – We were in town to-day. I got my nitted cap. It is brown & tan mixed. $2.75. Oscar bo't his leather jacket $8.50.

Nov. 18 – Carlton Christiansen shelled 450 bu of white corn to-day. We sold 6 loads for 27¢ a bu.

Nov. 22 – It has been cold & cloudy all day. We got all the cattle in the barn to-night. Also the sucking calf we put a lot of our pullets in the chicken house to-night. We put up our hard coal stove yesterday.

Page 158 – 1921 & 1922

Dec. 1 – It sure is nice weather to-day. It isn't cold. We got in 10 eggs Oscar hauled a load of corn for Sam Michaelsen to-day.

Nov. 17 – A 7 ½ lb boy was born to Mr. & Mrs. Walter Larsen near Emmetsburg. He is named Elliott Walter [93].

Nov. 30 – To-day Esther Kemp & Andy Christensen were married in Atlantic.

Dec. 7 – To-day Arthur Bamsey & Edithe Pauline Harden were married.

Dec. 7 – To-day little Arlene Christensen [94] daughter of Mr. & Mrs. Tom Christensen passed away at the home of her grandparents. She was 2 yrs & 9 mos old. The funeral was held Friday the 9th.

---

[93] This is my wife's father.
[94] Arlene Henrietta Christensen, 1919 – 1921, was buried at Cuppy's Grove according to Find-A-Grave Memorial # 93072665.

Dec. 14th – To-day is fine weather. The roads are very good. Oscar hauled on load of shelled corn for us yesterday & one in the afternoon for Roy. Corn is 31¢. He hauled hogs for Harold [Findlay?] to-day. We got 18 eggs in yesterday.

Dec. 23 – It is cold to-day & freezing hard. It snowed some. We went up to the school house to hear a Xmas program. It was real good. There are 12 pupils. Edna Sahl is teacher.

Dec. 31 – We were in town Harlan to-day. It was kinda cold. There is sale in Lemke's store. I got a blue coat trimmed with gray plush. I got it at half price $22.50. Ma bo't brown wool serge for $1.29 a yd. Mrs. Alex Smith is sewing it.

1922

Jan. 4 – Last night Guy Graves big new barn burned to the ground. It rained some. To-day it is snowing & drifting and is cold.

Jan. 21 – To-day is a little chilly. Ma & Oscar were in town to-day. Ma bro't her brown wool dress home & also her every day house dress.

Page 159 - 1922

Feb. 6 – It is cold to-day. We butchered a hog. 2 wks ago. I have had a sore hand for around 2 wks. We get in around 60 eggs a day.

Feb. 2 – Grandma Vinding [95] died to-day and will be buried the 8th.

Feb. 6 – An 8 ½ lb. baby boy was born to Mrs. & Mr. Frank Heilsen this morning. Frank Jr.

Feb. 13 – A 9 lb. boy was born to Mr. and Mrs. Howard Thompson to-day.

Feb. 21 – To-day is foggy. We got in 58 eggs.

Feb. 22 – It rained all day yesterday and during the night it started to freeze and snow a little. The new river is up.

---

[95] The term "Grandma" likely just reflects familiarity and age or a nickname, not a relationship. Martha's grandparents were Keldgords and Jensens, not Vindings. Maria K. Vinding, 1833 – 1922, was buried at Cuppy's Grove according to Find-A-Grave Memorial # 46702805.

Mar. 6 – It is snowing to-day but not very cold. We got in 61 eggs to-day.

Mar. 16 – To-day Clarence Tobias & Miss Georgia Shannon were married.

Mar. 16 – We got in 91 eggs. Eggs are 18¢.

Mar. 27 – I have the mumps now. I have had them 3 days. We got in 100 eggs to-day. Oscar took 24 dz eggs in town.

Apr. 6 – To-day Oscar took 48 dz of eggs to town. We got our second new Ford the 7th. We got $125 for the old one, 17 model.

Apr. 9 – To-day is nice weather. We gathered 125 eggs.

May 20 – To-day Truelson papered our front room. The paper with the flowered border. I cleaned the kitchen the 23rd . We have 175 little chickens. Last Friday the 19th [Rev.] E[dward] H. Rasmussen & wife were here for supper. We were in Harlan Sunday forenoon to hear him. He spoke in the Danish Baptist Church.

Page 160

June 2 – It has been fine weather to-day. The Center Twp. Picnic was held to-day. I oiled the kitchen floor to-day & finished washing windows on the outside. We cleaned the north room yesterday. I set out a few tomato plant to-night. Oscar has plowed 10 acres the first time.

June 5 – Yesterday was "Rally" day out at Cuppy's Grove. There was a large crowd. We were out in the afternoon. Rev. L[awrence] Thompson of Council Bluffs spoke in the forenoon. [Rev.] Jacob Vinding spoke in the evening.

June 17 – We were in town to-day. Mrs. P. Paulsen was buried. There was a large crowd. She died the 15th.

July 4 – It is fine weather to-day. We picked about 16 qts of raspberries. We picked about 100 qts this year & sold 62 qts at 30¢ a qt. There was a big celebration in Harlan to-day. Oscar was in all day.

July 8 – This forenoon (Sat) Jens Larsen's & I started on a trip up to Ruthven. We got up there about 6 o'clock. We came home the 13th. We stopped in the camping grounds in Storm Lake & ate dinner.

July 5 – To-day Helen Rorbeck [96] died at her home. She was 17 yrs old. She was buried from Cuppy's. Luverne Tobias [97] passed away at her home in Calif. Aug 3, 1922. She was 20 yrs. old

Page 161 – 1922

Aug. 9 – This evening it hailed & rained hard here. It stripped the corn some & spoiled the garden.

Aug. 17 – To-day Oscar & I were down to Fair. There was a large crowd. The performances were good.

Aug. 27 – To-day is nice weather. Uncle Charlie [Keldgord?] & Oscar started at 6 o'clock for Ruthven Ia. 130 mi. They are going to bring Mabel & children home for a visit.

Sept. 14 – To-day is fine weather, kinda cold. I canned snow apples to-day & Made plum jell. Mabel & children left on the 9

---

[96] Helen M. Rorbeck, 1905 – 1922, was buried at Cuppy's Grove according to Find-A-Grave Memorial # 98479813.
[97] LeVerne Tobias, 1902 – 1922, was buried at Forest Lawn Cemetery, Glendale, California according to Find-A-Grave Memorial # 117856212.

o'clock train for Ruthven to-day after spending nearly 3 wks at home.

July 6 – Mrs. Marinus Christensen [98] passed away to-day at her home in Harlan. She was 66 years old.

Oct. 1 – To-day is Sunday. Mama is sixty one yrs old to-day. We were in to Peter Petersen's. Mrs. Petersen's birthday is the 2nd. Thorvald & his wife & baby were there & Eddie & Moody Petersen were also there. Ma & I stayed there & went to church in the evening.

Page 162 – 1922

Oct. 4 – To-day Oscar went to town to get our new Quick Meal stove with white doors. We bo't it of Hans Hansen for $50.00.

Oct. 29 – We have picked corn for 2 wks. We have the crib full. The corn is sure dry, but there is a few moldy ears. The cows are going in the stalks to-morrow. We were to church to-day.

Oct. 24 – To-day Michael Hansen [99] passed away at his old home in Cuppy's Grove age 85 yrs & 10 mos.

Nov. 13 – To-day it rained all forenoon and all last night & yesterday. We picked corn every day last week. We just have 24 rows left in this piece behind the grove.

Dec. 10 – To-day is cold. We went to church. [Rev. Alexander V.] Hoiris preached. He has been here for 2 wks holding meetings. We were over to Adam's for dinner and also was to church in the evening.

---

[98] Anna C. Nasby Christensen, 1855 – 1922, was buried in the Harlan Cemetery according to Find-A-Grave Memorial # 27430754.
[99] Michael Hanson, Dec. 23, 1836 – Oct. 24, 1922, was buried at Cuppy's Grove according to Find-A-Grave Memorial # 98487905.

Dec. 11 – To-day we washed. It is very cold, about 10 above zero. Oscar went to town in the car. He took 2 dz of eggs in for 39¢ a dz.

We have our chickens shut up now. We have been getting about 10 eggs every day. We bo't 2 roosters of Ellis Gearhart this year.

Martha Keldgord's Journal 1911 - 1930

1923

Feb. 21 – To-day has been a fine day. Oscar helped Elmer Steels move to the Booth place east of town.

Page 163 – 1923

Jan. 15 – Cousin Eleanor Nelson [100] passed away at her home in Selma Calif. to-day of diphtheria age 6 yrs.

Feb. 23 – To-day a baby boy was born to Mr. & Mrs. Frank Heilesen (Donald).

March 8 – We were in [town?] to-day. The roads were muddy. I bo't my tan spring coat with tuxedo collar at Boysen & Lage for $23.50 and Oscar got his checked suit at Ben Griffith for $36.00.

Mar. 13 – To-day is cold & it snowed last night. Backs were up here yesterday. We got in 67 eggs yesterday.

Mar. 14 – To-day it is snowing & drifting and quite cold.

March 15 – It is a blizzard to-day. It blowed & snowed all night. We were down to Danielson's for dinner to-day after church. Mar. 11.

March 18 – To-day is Sunday. It is snowing & blowing & drifting and awfully cold. The cattle & horses have been in the barn all day.

July 8 - We have over 300 little chickens this year. It is "Rally" day in Harlan church to-day. Oscar went in a while this afternoon. Oscar finished plowing corn yesterday. We sold 9

---

[100] Eleanor Nelson was daughter of Rev. Nels Nelson and Florence.

sows yesterday at $15.50 a cwt. We are going to put up hay this week. I am going with Jim & Marie up north to-morrow morning. We were up there 1 wk. We were in a motor boat on Lost Island Lake the 15th a Sunday.

Page 164 – 1923

July 22 – We went to church in the morning. A Rev. Madsen spoke, from Eldora Ia. We were up to Frank Heilesen's for dinner. It was awfully hot to-day.

July 23 – John S. finished cutting our oats to-day. We are also thru making hay. John S. are going to thresh to-morrow.

Sept. 6 – To-day Uncle Nels came from Calif to Walnut. We went down after him. He staid here till the 18th. He preached in our church Sun the 9th & in the evening in Harlan. We were down to Arentsen's on Sunday.

Arentsen's 1923 - L to R - Stella Arentsen Mickelson, George Mickelson, Harold Mickelson, Annie Arentsen, Mary Arentsen, Oscar Keldgord, Martina Keldgord, Martha Keldgord, Nels Nelson (family photo.)

Sept. 7 – We were in town to-day. Uncle Nels was also along. Mama bo't some new glasses of Mr. Griffith in Tinsleys for $12.00.

Nov. 21 – To-day we finished picking corn about 34 acres. We have our crib full & double cribbing full. We have had nice weather for corn picking.

Dec. 1 – We bo't a Fuller hair brush with dark handle & a duster with handle to-day.

1926 – 1930

Feb. 1926 – Our first radio. We bo't our Freshman Masterpiece Radio at Harlan's Drug store.

Jan. 31, 1927 – We bo't our new black horse in Avoca to-day for $115. Her name is Belle.

Dec. 18, 1930 – A baby girl was born to Frank Heilesens to-day named Evelyn. [The following appears to be added at a later date.] Now Mrs. Jacobsen.

[The remainder of the journal, pages 165 – 178, consists of poems.]

Martha Keldgord's Journal 1911 - 1930

Afterword

Martha continued to write her journals. There are two more, one dated October 9, 1934 running into 1948, and another dated March 12, 1948 and running into 1967. She continued to live at home with her brother, Oscar, and mother, Martine, for most of that time. Her mother died in 1955 and Oscar died in 1959, leaving her alone on the farm. She moved into Harlan for a short time prior to marrying Walter Larsen in 1960. Walter had been married to Martha's sister, Mabel, until her death in 1958. Martha lived in Graettinger, Iowa, until her death in 1979 at the age of 84.

Martha and Walter Larsen, granddaughter Irene – 1960 (family photo)

Martha Keldgord's Journal 1911 - 1930

Index of Places

Martha Keldgord's Journal 1911 - 1930

Index of People

Rev. Julius A., 93, 97,
  105, 111, 116, 117, 118
Rev. Ralph, 73, 111
Soren, 34, 50, 54, 99, 117,
  124
Thule, 78
Jespersen
  P., 69
Johnson
  Chris, 117
  Clarence, 103, 106
  Emma, 103
  Nellie, 108
  Otellie, 117
Jorgens
  Nora, 114
Jorgensen
  Jacob, 118
  Nora, 115
Keldgord
  Anna, 8
  Carl, 62
  Charlie, Uncle, 62, 129
  Chris, 8, 31
  Clarence, 31
  Elmer, 86
  Elmer and Sue, 89, 94
  Marianne Jacobsdatter, 1
  Olga, 1
  Peter Christensen, 1
Keldgord Hollenbeck
  Mary, Aunt, 58
Kemp, 79, 83
  Arla May, 118
  Esther, 7, 125
  Howard Edwin, 102
  James, 79

Kenneth, 117
Paul, 72, 73, 85, 102, 118
Kern
  Miss, 79
Kimball
  Senator, 70
Kjeldgaard
  Cathrine, 25
  Clara, 25, 40
  Cristine, 25
  Svante, 23, 24, 25, 29, 37,
    40, 73
  Swante, 27
Kjer
  Claus, 61
  Karl, 70
Klindts, 47
  Rudolf, 48, 55
Klitgard
  Andrew, 103
Knudson/en
  Ann, 105
  Anna, 9
  Arthur, 73
  Arthur S., 73
  C., 75
  Mrs. Soren,old, 105
Krogh, 13
Lansman
  Charlie, 53, 68
Lapham, Dr., 47
Larsen
  Beathe, 34, 106
  Carl, 54
  Ed, 65, 73
  Edwin, 63, 104
  Elliott Walter, 125

Elmer, 85, 122, 133
Stofferson
  C., 11
Svensen, 78
Swenson
  C. Anton, 65
T.
  Clifford, 114
Taylor
  Alma, 17
Therkelsen
  George, 55
Thompson
  Howard, 75, 76, 127
  Rev. Lawrence, 128
Thorgesen
  Chris, 77
Tobias
  Clarence, 80, 128
  Daisy, 80
  Luverne, 129
Trennery
  Rev., 77
Troll
  Lulu, 114
Truelson, 49, 128
Tucker, 92

Turner
  Mrs., 93
V.
  Chester, 114
Vinding
  Grandma, 127
  John, 70, 120
  Rev. Jacob D., 94, 109,
    128
Weber
  Bernice, 35, 39
  Leo, 40
  Leo and Marie, 20, 23, 25,
    29, 35, 36, 39
Wesgard
  Rev. Martin A., 118, 119
  Rev. Martin.A., 74
White
  Ed, 70
Wilcox
  Dr., 49
Wilson, 39, 47, 49, 84, 85,
  92, 108
Wyland
  Mary Jane, 102, 103

References

Altamont Baptist Church. *Sixtieth Anniversary of the Altamont Baptist Church of Cuppy's Grove, Harlan, Iowa.* Harlan, Iowa: Altamont Baptist Church, 1930.

Cowden, Virginia M. Bisgard. *I Shook Our Family Tree.* Des Moines, Iowa: Privately printed, 1987.

Danish Baptist General Conference of America. *Seventy-five Years of Danish Baptist Missionary Work in America.* The Judson Press, 1931.

FamilySearch. California Birth Index. <http://familysearch.org> 2013. (2013).

FamilySearch. California Death Index. <http://familysearch.org> 2013. (2013).

Find A Grave, Inc. Find A Grave.com. <http://www.findagrave.com>: 2013.

Geo. A. Ogle & Co, compiler. Standard Atlas of Shelby County Iowa.Chicago, Illinois:Geo. A. Ogle & Co., 1911.

Henry Doorly Zoo. History. <http://www.omahazoo.com/about/history> 2013. (2013).

Iowa Shelby County. 1900 U.S. census, population schedule. Ancestry.com. 2013.(2013).

Iowa, Shelby County. 1910 U.S.census, population schedule. Ancestry.com. 2013. (2013).

Iowa, Shelby County. 1920 U.S.census, population schedule. Ancestry.com. 2013. (2013).

Iowa, Shelby County. 1925 Iowa State Census. Ancestry.com 2013. (2013).

Knights of Ak-Sar-Ben Foundation. History.
<http://www.aksarben.org/history2> 2013. (2013).

Mesenbrink, Bob. *The Ancestors of Walter and Mabel (Keldgord) Larsen.* Arvada, Colorado: Privately printed, 2009.

New York, New York City. 1910 U.S. census, population schedule. Ancestry.com. 2013. (2013).

New York City Department of Records and Information Services, Municipal Archives. Mary E. Hollenbeck death certificate, #17925. 1917.

White, Edward S. *The Past and Present of Shelby County, Iowa.* Indianapolis, Indiana: B.F. Bowen, 1915.

www.ingramcontent.com/pod-product-compliance
Lightning Source LLC
LaVergne TN
LVHW011234080426
835509LV00005B/496